Study Guide

GCSE Success

Spanish

Spanish

GCSE Success

Terry Murray

Contents

This book and

Stay on course! Use these pages to get to know your course.

No matter which exam board you are using, you have to do…
- a listening and a reading exam
- two controlled writing assessments
- two controlled speaking assessments.

For your listening and reading exams, your teacher will enter you for either Foundation or Higher:
- If you do Higher, your grade for that skill will be from A* to E.
- If you do Foundation, your grade for that skill will be from C to G.

In your speaking and writing controlled assessments, you are not entered for Foundation or Higher. Your final mark in these controlled assessments depends on how well you do. This is called 'differentiation by outcome'.

Here are some guidelines on the length of the exams and controlled assessments:

Listening Foundation
An exam lasting 30–40 minutes.
Listening Higher
An exam lasting 40–50 minutes.
Reading Foundation
An exam lasting 30–40 minutes.
Reading Higher
An exam lasting 40–50 minutes.
Speaking
Two controlled assessments lasting four to six minutes each.
Writing
Two controlled assessments lasting about an hour each.

Individual exam boards' topic areas are shown opposite. You should revise all the topics relevant to your specification but it will help to build your vocabulary and improve your Spanish if you also study the other topics.

AQA

Lifestyle
Health:
- Healthy and unhealthy lifestyles and their consequences

Relationships and choices:
- Relationships with family and friends
- Future plans regarding marriage/partnership
- Social issues and equality

Leisure
Free time and the media:
- Free time activities
- Shopping, money, fashion and trends
- Advantages and disadvantages of new technology

Holidays:
- Plans, preferences, experiences
- What to see and getting around

Home and environment
Home and local area:
- Special occasions celebrated in the home
- Home, town, neighbourhood and region; where it is and what it is like

Environment:
- Current problems facing the planet
- Being environmentally friendly within the home and local area

Work and education
School/college and future plans:
- What school/college is like
- Pressures and problems

Current and future jobs:
- Looking for and getting a job
- Advantages and disadvantages of different jobs

OCR

Topic area 1 – Home and local area
- Life in the home, friends and relationships
- Local area, facilities and getting around

Topic area 2 – Health and sport
- Sport, outdoor pursuits and healthy lifestyle
- Food and drink as aspects of culture and health

Topic area 3 – Leisure and entertainment (includes online)
- Socialising, special occasions and festivals
- TV, films and music

Topic area 4 – Travel and the wider world
- Holidays and exchanges
- Environmental, cultural and social issues

Topic area 5 – Education and work
- School life in the UK and in the target language country or community
- Work experience, future study and jobs, working abroad

Visit your awarding body's website for full course details or download your complete GCSE specifications.

your GCSE course

EDEXCEL

Speaking and writing
1. Media and culture
- Music/film/reading
- Fashion/celebrities/religion
- Blogs/Internet

2. Sport and leisure
- Hobbies/interests
- Sporting events
- Lifestyle choices

3. Travel and tourism
- Holidays
- Accommodation
- Eating, food, drink

4. Business, work and employment
- Work experience/part-time jobs
- Product or service information

5. Centre-devised option

Listening and reading
Out and about
- Visitor information
- Basic weather
- Local amenities
- Accommodation
- Public transport
- Directions

Customer service and transactions
- Cafés and restaurants
- Shops
- Dealing with problems

Personal information
- General interests
- Leisure activities
- Family and friends
- Lifestyle (healthy eating and exercise)

Future plans, education and work
- Basic language of the Internet
- Simple job advertisements
- Simple job applications and CVs
- School and college
- Work and work experience

WJEC

Personal and social life
- Self, family, friends, home life, shopping, meals, healthy living, illness and accidents, free time, fashion, relationships, future plans.

Local community
- Home town, school, education, local environment, pollution, recycling, local facilities, comparisons with other towns and regions, weather and seasons.

The world of work
- Work experience, part-time jobs, future careers, technology (sending messages, accessing information).

The wider world
- Travel and holidays, media, social issues (e.g. life of young people today, homelessness, crime, drugs, healthy living, religion, politics), life in the countries and communities where the language is spoken.

CCEA

Context 1: The individual
– Students' lives, families, homes and interests, and those of others in Spanish-speaking countries and communities
- Relationships: families and friends
- Local environment: advantages and disadvantages
- Activities: daily routine and leisure activities
- Health and lifestyle: diet, exercise and illness

Context 2: Citizenship
– Lifestyles, attitudes and customs in students' own countries and communities, and in Spanish-speaking countries and communities
- Social issues: problems in society and equality
- Travel and tourism: destinations and choices
- Environmental issues: attitudes to and responsibilities for litter, transport, energy, conservation and recycling
- Media and communications
- Celebrations: festivals and customs

Context 3: Employability
– Education and employment in students' own countries and communities, and in Spanish-speaking countries and communities
- School life
- Part-time jobs: advantages and disadvantages
- Future plans: choices and expectations

www.aqa.org.uk, www.ocr.org.uk, www.edexcel.com, www.wjec.co.uk, www.ccea.org.uk

A student's guide to the speaking and writing controlled assessments

How many controlled assessments do I have to do?
Two for speaking and two for writing.

When will I be doing my controlled assessments?
Anytime in Year 9, 10 or 11. Your teacher can choose the time.

How long are the controlled assessments?
Each speaking assessment will last four to six minutes (WJEC: four to seven minutes). The writing assessment will be a minimum of 200 words, spread over the two pieces, but you should aim for 400–600 words, spread over the two pieces, if you want at least a grade C. Each writing assessment must be done in an hour.

When do I start preparing?
There are three stages:

Stage 1: Your teacher will prepare you for the task. He/she cannot tell you at this stage what the task is.
Stage 2: The teacher gives you the task. After this, the teacher cannot give you any language guidance, but he/she can tell you that past tenses are to be used here and future tenses there, for example. Stage 2 can last for anything from a few days to most of a term, depending on the exam board:

AQA	Six hours including lesson time and homework time
OCR	Two hours of class time
EDEXCEL	Speaking: two weeks and no more than six hours of contact time Writing: No limit
WJEC	Two weeks
CCEA	Speaking: three to four hours. Writing: five to six hours

Stage 3: This is when you do the controlled assessment.

Can I ask my teacher to extend the deadline?
No.

What if I do an awful piece of controlled assessment?
Your teacher will let you do another one but it must be a different task.

Can I use ICT?
In the controlled writing assessment, you can write your work on a computer but it will take place in exam conditions.

It is very clear that many GCSE candidates write less well using ICT. In particular, they tend to be less accurate and leave out more accents when they type. So use word-processing with care.

Can I use electronic translators?
No. In the controlled speaking assessment, you will have access to your cue card of 30–40 words. In the controlled writing assessment, you will have access to your cue card of 30–40 words and a dictionary. This can be an online dictionary.

You should always take care to make all your work neat and easy to read.

Do I get marks for presentation?
No – if you write a brochure, for example, you will not get any marks for pictures and maps (even if you draw them yourself). Similarly, do not waste time on title pages, fancy borders, folders and so on.

Can I do the same piece of speaking or writing as other people in my class?
Yes, and you will probably use quite a lot of the same vocabulary and structures as well. But there will always be differences as you will be speaking or writing about your holiday or your work experience, for example.

Can I use a writing frame?

In Stage 1 and 2, yes. However, the more of your own ideas you write, the higher your marks are likely to be.

Can I use pieces of writing I have seen in books?

You must never, ever copy. However, you should try to use lots of interesting vocabulary and phrases you have learned from your worksheets and coursebooks.

Can I get other people to help me?

No – you and your teacher have to sign that this is your own, unaided controlled assessment. You will cover all of the language you need in class and you will be helped with your planning. Your teacher will have a good idea of the standard of writing you are capable of from your other work in class. If your teacher suspects you have not written a piece of controlled assessment yourself, he/she might...

- refuse to let you submit it at all
- make you rewrite the piece in exam conditions
- inform the exam board that you have been cheating.

Planning your study

Make sure that you have learned all the necessary words after you complete each topic. You could draw a mind map or create a database on your PC. During the topic try to learn 10 new words a day. Ask someone to test you on the words: you need to be able to spell the words properly, and use accents correctly, so remember to write them down when being tested.

- Each chapter in the book includes sample conversations. These conversations will help you to prepare for your controlled assessments in speaking. You might like to read the conversations with a friend and/or make a recording of the conversations. You could then listen to the conversations as part of your revision plan. This will boost your fluency.
- Practise the questions in the book. This will build your confidence and enable you to anticipate the type of questions that will occur in the GCSE examination.
- Decide if you know the topic thoroughly and if there are any weak areas: note them and look for ways to improve on them in the next topic, e.g. use of adjectives, use of the past tense.

How this book will help you

This Letts *Revise GCSE Spanish Study and Revision Guide* will help you because...

- it contains the essential vocabulary and grammatical structures needed for the GCSE course.
- it contains progress checks as well as GCSE questions to help you to check and reaffirm your understanding.
- there are examples of controlled assessment tasks with model answers and advice from an examiner on how to get them right. Translations are provided on pages 155–156 to aid understanding.
- trying the exam practice questions will give you the opportunity to make use of the vocabulary that you have learned and will give you a measure of your progress.
- examiner's hints and key points are used throughout the chapters to help you. Use these as your signposts to guide you to success in your GCSE course.

32 points for improving your grade

Do not try to include all 32 points – 15 to 20 will be fine.

Listed below are 32 points that will help to improve the quality of language in your speaking and writing work and raise your grade in the controlled assessments. Try to include a good number of these points in your work.

Examples of these points being used are shown where you see this icon , on the 'Sample controlled assessment' pages throughout this book.

1 Use a **tener** structure, e.g.:

tener ganas de	to want to
Tengo ganas de ir a Francia.	I want to go to France.
tener suerte	to be lucky
Tenía suerte porque...	I was lucky because...

2 Try to include at least three uses of **porque**, e.g.:

Fui a Francia porque me gusta la cocina.
I went to France because I like the food.

3 Try to include at least two justified points of view, e.g.:

Creo que España es el mejor país del mundo porque la cocina es tan buena.
I think that Spain is the best country in the world because the food is so good.

4 Use **decidí** + the infinitive (I decided to...)

5 Use **sin** + the infinitive, e.g.:

sin perder un momento	without wasting a moment

6 Use **antes de...**, e.g.:

antes de llegar	before arriving
antes de comer	before eating

7 Use **al** + the infinitive, e.g.:

al llegar	on arriving
al verle	on seeing him

8 Use **después de** + the infinitive, e.g.:

Después de comer, fui...	After eating, I went...

9 Use exclamations, e.g.:

¡Qué buena idea!	What a good idea!
¡Qué desastre!	What a disaster!

10 Try to include at least three uses of the present tense, including an irregular.

11 Try to include at least three preterites, including an irregular and a reflexive.

12 Try to include at least three future tenses, including an irregular.

13 Use an imperfect, e.g.:

Llovía.	It was raining.

14 Use a conditional, e.g.:

sería	I would be

15 Use adjectives, e.g.:

inolvidable	unforgettable
desgraciado	unfortunate

16 Use impressive vocabulary and structures, e.g.:

Dejé de fumar.	I stopped smoking.
Empiezo a...	I begin to...

17 Use a pluperfect (i.e. had done something), e.g.:

Ya le había conocido antes.	I had already met him before.
que me habían prometido	that I had been promised

18 Use **verdaderamente**, **tan** and **extremadamente** instead of **muy**, e.g.:

verdaderamente importante	truly/really important

19 Use **a pesar de** (in spite of), e.g.:

A pesar de que no tengo dinero...
In spite of the fact that I have no money...

20 Use **acabar de** (to have just), e.g.:

Acabo de empezar una nueva lengua.
I have just started a new language.

21 Use **estar a punto de** (to be on the point of/about to), e.g.:

Estaba a punto de hacer mis deberes...
I was just about to do my homework...

22 Use comparatives, e.g.:

más guapo que	more handsome than
menos fuerte que	less strong than
tan inteligente como	as intelligent as
no es tan bonita como	not as pretty as

23 Use superlatives, e.g.:

la más bonita	the prettiest
el más desagradable	the most unpleasant

24 Use negatives, e.g.:

No voy nunca.	I never go.

25 Try to include a subjunctive (this is an A-level structure but you can get extra marks by using examples), e.g.:

Esperemos que sí.	Let's hope so.
Ojalá pudiera.	If only I could.

26 Use **desde hace** (since), e.g.:

Vivo aquí desde hace 15 años.	I have lived here for 15 years.

27 Try to reduce the number of simple verbs, such as **me llamo**, **tengo** and **es**.

28 Try to use full descriptions (i.e. 10 pieces of information).

29 Try not to repeat any verb.

30 Use connecting words (connectives), e.g.:

que	who, which, that
mientras	whilst, whereas
porque	for, because
cuando	when
puesto que	since

31 Use **para** + the infinitive, e.g.:

Para ver a mi amigo...	In order to see my friend...

32 Use pronouns, e.g.:

Me acompañó mi hermano mayor.	My older brother came with me.

In the piece of work below, the student has implemented most of the 32 points. This piece of work would be worth an A*. The numbers in the text refer to the points outlined on pages 8–9.

School

The '32 points for improving your grade' are referenced in the passages on the 'Sample controlled assessment' pages in the same way as they appear in this example.

Por desgracia[16] tengo que[1] irme a la cama a las nueve para poder[31] levantarme a las seis. Al levantarme,[7] me ducho y después de desayunar,[8] salgo lo antes posible[23] a coger el autobús. Acabo de conocer[20] a Pedro y me[32] acompaña normalmente. Lo conozco desde hace dos semanas.[26] Al llegar,[7] me encuentro con mis amigos y tengo cinco clases. Historia, no la aguanto más.[24]

Ayer en el instituto ¡qué desastre![9] Estaba a punto de[21] empezar mi primera clase – la peor asignatura[23] – historia – cuando descubrí que había dejado[17] todos mis libros en casa. Sin perder un momento,[5] llamé a mi hermano mayor[16] y los[32] trajo en el coche.

Pero el profe me regañó.[16] Tenía miedo.[1] El profe es tan severo.[18] Decidí[4] dejar la asignatura puesto que el profe me regaña continuamente.

Mañana tendré[12] mi asignatura preferida – español. Creo que es la asignatura más importante porque el español es verdaderamente útil[18] para todo el mundo. Un día seré[12] profe de español. Eso sería maravilloso...[14]

Tips for listening and reading

In the listening exam, first read the question carefully and highlight the question word so that you know the information that you are listening for. Use any visuals to help you to predict what you might hear. Try to anticipate the answer and note down possible words to listen for. Check numbers, dates and times very carefully.

In the reading exam, read the questions before you read the passage. Some words look like English words – you should try to work out their meaning.

It pays to think logically in both the reading and listening exams. Sometimes you have to use your common sense to work out the answers from the information given.

Examiners will also test your knowledge of synonyms and related families of words, e.g. **A Susi le gusta leer** may become **A Susi le encanta la lectura**. Ensure that you know synonyms and families of nouns and verbs. Make a list of synonyms, near-synonyms and word families and learn them carefully, e.g. **el salón** = **la sala de estar**.

1 Lifestyle and health

The following topics are covered in this chapter:

- Healthy and unhealthy lifestyles
- Food and drink
- Accidents and incidents
- Grammar

1.1 Healthy and unhealthy lifestyles

LEARNING SUMMARY

After studying this section, you should be able to:

- describe how to keep fit and healthy
- talk about your diet

Healthy lifestyles

AQA ✓
OCR ✓
EDEXCEL ✓
WJEC ✓
CCEA ✓

The following sentences contain vocabulary and structures that will help you in the listening and reading exams, and in the controlled assessment.

Lifestyles

> Note how many of the sentences in 'Lifestyles' tend to start with different structures. Using a variety of structures gains extra marks in the controlled assessments.

He aquí unos consejos para mantenerte en forma y evitar enfermedades.
Some advice about staying fit and avoiding illness.

Hay que evitar enfermedades llevando un estilo de vida sana.
We must avoid illness by leading a healthy lifestyle.

Una dieta poco saludable causa enfermedades del corazón y miles de muertos.
An unhealthy diet causes heart disease and thousands of deaths.

Un joven de cada seis es obeso.
One child in six is obese.

Voy a comer una dieta sana.
I am going to eat a healthy diet.

Voy a variar lo que como.
I will vary my diet.

La cantidad de fruta y verdura que como es importante.
The amount of fruit and vegetables I eat is important.

Comeré por lo menos cinco porciones de fruta y verdura al día.
I will eat at least five portions of fruit and vegetables a day.

Voy a hacer ejercicio regularmente.
I will exercise regularly.

Evitaré comida basura y materia grasa.

I will avoid junk food and fat.

No debo fumar.

I must not smoke.

Tengo que acostarme temprano.

I should go to bed early.

Quiero dormir ocho horas como mínimo.

I want to sleep for a minimum of eight hours.

No voy a beber alcohol.

I am not going to drink alcohol.

Quiero cambiar mi estilo de vida.

I would like to change the way I live.

Quiero ir al gimnasio, hacer ejercicio y jugar al fútbol.

I want to go to the gym, do exercise and play football.

Quiero comer comida más sana y llevar una dieta equilibrada.

I want to eat healthier food and have a balanced diet.

Prefiero comer más zanahorias, tomar vitaminas y evitar grasas y patatas fritas.

I would prefer to eat more carrots, take vitamins and avoid fat and chips.

No debemos pasar horas enteras viendo la tele.

You must not spend too much time watching TV.

No debemos alimentarnos con comida basura.

You must not just live off junk food.

Hay que salir al aire libre.

You must get out into the open air.

PROGRESS CHECK

Say or write the following in Spanish:

1. A balanced diet
2. The open air
3. Healthier food
4. I must not smoke.
5. Avoid illness.

1. Una dieta equilibrada
2. El aire libre
3. Comida más sana
4. No debo fumar.
5. Evitar enfermedades.

1.2 Food and drink

LEARNING SUMMARY

After studying this section, you should be able to:

- talk about food and drink
- say what you like and do not like to eat and drink

Eating and drinking

AQA	✓
OCR	✓
EDEXCEL	✓
WJEC	✓
CCEA	✓

The topic of food and drink is regularly tested in listening and reading exams. In the controlled speaking assessment, you might have to talk about what food and drink you like and dislike.

Meals (Las comidas)

el almuerzo, la comida – lunch
la cena – evening meal

el desayuno – breakfast
la merienda – snack, picnic

Vegetables (Las verduras)

el ajo – garlic
el arroz – rice
la cebolla – onion
el champiñon – mushroom
la col – cabbage
las coles de Bruselas – Brussels sprouts
la coliflor – cauliflower
la ensalada – salad
el espárrago – asparagus
las espinacas – spinach

el guisante – pea
el haba (f) – bean
las judías verdes – green beans
la lechuga – lettuce
las legumbres – vegetables
la patata – potato
las patatas fritas – chips
el pepino – cucumber
el pimiento (verdura) – pepper
el tomate – tomato
la zanahoria – carrot

la cebolla

Fruit (La fruta)

el albaricoque – apricot
la cereza – cherry
la ciruela – plum
la frambuesa – raspberry
la fresa – strawberry
el limón – lemon
la manzana – apple

el melocotón – peach
el melón – melon
la naranja – orange
la pera – pear
la piña – pineapple
el plátano – banana
la uva – grape

la piña

Meat (La carne)

el bistec – steak
la carne de vaca – beef
el cerdo – pork
el cordero – lamb
el chorizo – Spanish sausage

la chuleta – chop
el jamón – ham
el pollo – chicken
la ternera – veal

el jamón

On the table (En la mesa)

el azúcar – sugar
el bol – bowl
la cafetera – coffeepot
el cubierto – cutlery, place setting
la cuchara – spoon
el cuchillo – knife
el mantel – tablecloth
la mesa – table
la mostaza – mustard
la pimienta – pepper

el platillo – saucer
el plato – dish
la sal – salt
la salsa – sauce, gravy
la servilleta – serviette, napkin
la taza – cup
el tenedor – fork
el vaso – glass
el vinagre – vinegar

la cuchara

Snacks and other food (Tentempiés y otra comida)

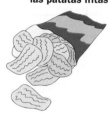

las patatas fritas

la barra – loaf
el bizcocho – biscuit
el bocadillo – sandwich
los bombones – chocolates
los caramelos – sweets
el chocolate – chocolate

el churro – fritter
la galleta – biscuit
la hamburguesa – hamburger
la harina – flour
el huevo – egg

el panecillo – roll
las patatas fritas – crisps
el perrito caliente – hot dog
la salchicha – sausage
la tortilla – omelette

Fish and seafood (El pescado y los mariscos)

el bacalao – cod
los calamares – squid
el cangrejo – crab

las gambas – prawns
la langosta – lobster
los mejillones – mussels

el salmón – salmon
la sardina – sardine
la trucha – trout

Desserts (Los postres)

el helado

el helado – ice cream
la nata – cream

el pastel – cake
el queso – cheese

la tarta – cake
el yogur – yoghurt

Breakfast (El desayuno)

los cereales – cereals
el huevo pasado por agua – boiled egg
la mantequilla – butter
la mermelada – jam
la mermelada de naranja – marmalade

la miel – honey
el pan – bread
el pan tostado – toasted bread
la tostada – toast

Drinks (Las bebidas)

el café

el agua (f) – water
el agua mineral con gas – mineral water (fizzy)
el agua mineral sin gas – mineral water (still)
el café – coffee
la cerveza – beer
la Coca-Cola – Coca-Cola
la gaseosa – lemonade
el jugo de fruta – fruit juice

la leche – milk
la limonada – lemonade
la naranjada – orangeade
el refresco – soft drink
el té – tea
el tinto – red wine
el vino – wine
el zumo de fruta – fruit juice
el zumo de naranja – orange juice

Conversation: Grade C

AQA ✓
OCR ✓
EDEXCEL ✓
WJEC ✓
CCEA ✓

🔵 **¿Para desayunar?¿Qué comes y qué bebes?**
⚪ Bebo café con leche y como pan tostado con un huevo.
🔵 **¿Qué fruta prefieres?**
⚪ Prefiero las manzanas.

¿Tienes una carne favorita?

Prefiero el pollo.

¿Qué legumbre prefieres?

Prefiero las patatas fritas.

En un café, ¿qué comes y qué bebes?

Normalmente bebo Coca-Cola y como un perrito caliente.

¿Te gustan los helados?

Claro.

¿Qué tipo de helado prefieres?

Prefiero el helado de fresa.

De postre, ¿qué prefieres?

Prefiero una tarta o un pastel con nata.

¿Te gusta el queso?

Odio el queso. Prefiero los dulces.

¿Qué te gusta beber?

Para desayunar bebo té. En un café bebo cerveza.

¿Te gusta el vino?

Me gusta el vino blanco pero no me gusta el vino tinto.

¿Qué has comido hoy?

Esta mañana comí panecillos y esta tarde voy a comer un bistec.

In restaurants and cafés

AQA	✓
OCR	✓
EDEXCEL	✓
WJEC	✓
CCEA	✓

In a restaurant (En un restaurante)

los aseos – toilets

el/la camarero/a – waiter/waitress

la comida – food

la especialidad – speciality

el menú del día – menu of the day

el plato combinado – set meal

por aquí – this way

la receta – recipe

el sabor – flavour

el servicio – service

los servicios – toilets

el/la vegetariano/a – vegetarian

el vaso

In a café (En una cafetería)

la bandeja – tray

el café con leche – white coffee

el café solo – black coffee

la cuenta – bill

el hielo – ice

el mostrador – counter

nada más – that's all

la propina – tip

la ración – portion

la sombra – shade

las tapas – bar snacks

el vaso – glass

Restaurant verbs

almorzar, comer – to have lunch

beber – to drink

cenar – to have dinner

comer – to eat

desayunar – to have breakfast

merendar – to have a snack/picnic

pagar – to pay

pedir – to ask for, to order

probar – to try out

1.3 Accidents and incidents

LEARNING SUMMARY	After studying this section, you should be able to:
	• describe your own (or someone else's) state of health
	• refer to particular health problems
	• explain how accidents happened
	• describe incidents such as theft

Health

AQA	✓
OCR	✓
EDEXCEL	✓
WJEC	✓
CCEA	✓

The topic health is frequently examined in the listening and reading exams. It may also figure in your controlled assessment for speaking and writing.

el ojo · el pelo · la oreja · la nariz · la mejilla · la boca · el cuello

The body (El cuerpo)

la barba – beard	**la espalda** – back	**la nariz** – nose
la barbilla – chin	**el estómago** – stomach	**el ojo** – eye
el bigote – moustache	**la frente** – forehead	**la oreja** – ear
la boca – mouth	**la garganta** – throat	**el pelo** – hair (on head or body)
el brazo – arm	**el hombro** – shoulder	
el cabello – hair (on head)	**el hueso** – bone	**el pie** – foot
la cabeza – head	**el labio** – lip	**la piel** – skin
la cara – face	**la lágrima** – tear	**la pierna** – leg
el codo – elbow	**la lengua** – tongue	**la rodilla** – knee
el corazón – heart	**la mano** – hand	**el rostro** – face
el cuello – neck	**la mejilla** – cheek	**el tobillo** – ankle
el dedo – finger	**la muela** – tooth (molar)	**el vientre** – stomach
el diente – tooth	**la muñeca** – wrist	**la voz** – voice

Health and illnesses (La salud y las enfermedades)

la **ambulancia** – ambulance
la **aspirina** – aspirin
el **catarro** – cold
la **cita** – appointment (e.g. with doctor)
la **clínica** – clinic
el **comprimido** – tablet
el **consultorio** – doctor's surgery
la **crema** – cream
la **cura** – cure
el **dolor** – pain
el **dolor de cabeza** – headache
el **dolor de muelas** – toothache
la **droga** – drug
el **empaste** – filling
el **esparadrapo** – sticking plaster
la **farmacia** – chemist's
la **fiebre** – temperature
la **gripe** – flu
la **herida** – wound

el **hospital** – hospital
la **insolación** – sunstroke
la **inyección** – injection
el **medicamento** – medicine
la **medicina** – medicine
la **operación** – operation
la **pastilla** – tablet
la **picadura** – bite (insect)
la **quemadura** – burn
la **receta** – prescription
el **remedio** – remedy
el **resfriado** – cold
el **sida** – Aids
el **síntoma** – symptom
la **tirita** – sticking plaster
la **tos** – cough
el **tratamiento** – treatment
la **venda** – bandage

la gripe

la operación

guardar cama

People (La gente)

el/la **dentista** – dentist
el/la **doctor(a)** – doctor
el/la **enfermero/a** – nurse

el/la **farmacéutico/a** – chemist
el/la **médico** – doctor

Verbs

cortar – to cut
desmayarse – to faint
doler – to hurt
estar bien – to feel OK
estar constipado – to have a cold
estar mal – to feel ill
guardar cama – to stay in bed
mantenerse – to maintain
marearse – to get dizzy/seasick
picar – to bite, to sting

quemarse – to burn oneself
remediar – to put right
resbalar – to slip
sentirse – to feel
temblar – to tremble
torcer – to turn, to twist
toser – to cough
vendar – to bandage
vomitar – to vomit

Accidents and incidents

AQA ✓
OCR ✓
EDEXCEL ✓
WJEC ✓
CCEA ✓

The following vocabulary will help you in the listening and reading exams, and in the controlled assessment.

Accidents/incidents (Los accidentes/los incidentes)

la ambulancia – ambulance
el asesinato – murder
el atraco – hold-up, mugging
la aventura – adventure
el aviso – warning
la ayuda – help
la bomba – bomb
la cárcel – prison
el choque – collision
el crimen – crime
el daño – damage
el desastre – disaster
la descripción – description
la desgracia – misfortune
la escena – scene
el fuego – fire
el fusil – rifle
el golpe – blow

el grito – shout
el humo – smoke
el incendio – fire
la inundación – flood
la mentira – lie
la multa – fine
el peligro – danger
la pérdida – loss
el pinchazo – puncture, flat tyre
la recompensa – reward
el rescate – rescue
el riesgo – risk
el robo – robbery
la sangre – blood
el secuestro – kidnapping
el testigo – witness
la tragedia – tragedy
la vida – life

la inundación

el bombero

robar

People (La gente)

el/la asesino/a – murderer
el/la bombero/a – firefighter
el/la drogadicto/a – drug addict
el/la ladrón (-ona) – thief, burglar

el/la policía – police officer
la policía – police
el/la ratero/a – pickpocket
la víctima – victim

Verbs

ahogarse – to drown
apagar – to put out (e.g. a fire)
asesinar – to murder
atacar – to attack
atropellar – to run over
chocar (con) – to collide (with)
cometer – to commit
cruzar – to cross
desaparecer – to disappear
describir – to describe
golpear – to hit

gritar – to shout
herirse – to get injured
ocurrir – to happen
parar – to stop
pegar – to hit
rescatar – to rescue
robar – to steal
romperse – to break
salvar – to save
secuestrar – to kidnap
suceder – to happen

Conversation

AQA ✓
OCR ✓
EDEXCEL ✓
WJEC ✓
CCEA ✓

- ¿Qué tal las vacaciones?
- Mal. Estaba enfermo/a.
- ¿Qué te pasaba?
- Tenía dolor de estómago.
- ¿Fuiste a ver al médico?
- Sí, me dio una receta.

- ¿Viste el accidente?
- Sí, hubo una colisión entre un coche y un camión.
- ¿Hubo heridos?
- El camionero se rompió el brazo y el conductor del coche se cortó la cara.

PROGRESS CHECK

Say or write the following in Spanish:

1. Heart
2. Sunstroke
3. Nurse
4. To stay in bed
5. Murder
6. Firefighter
7. To drown
8. I have a headache.
9. I have a cold.
10. I have toothache.
11. I must stay in bed.

1. El corazón 2. La insolación 3. El/la enfermero/a 4. Guardar cama 5. El asesinato 6. El/la bombero/a 7. Ahogarse 8. Tengo dolor de cabeza. 9. Tengo un resfriado. 10. Tengo dolor de muelas. 11. Tengo que guardar cama.

1.4 Grammar

LEARNING SUMMARY

After studying this section, you should be able to understand:

- grammatical terms
- definite and indefinite articles
- nouns

Grammatical terms

AQA ✓
OCR ✓
EDEXCEL ✓
WJEC ✓
CCEA ✓

Before you start your grammar revision, you need to familiarise yourself with some grammatical terms. You will find this section useful to refer back to.

Look at this sentence:

The girl quickly makes a delicious cake in the kitchen.

The	definite article
girl	noun (subject)
quickly	adverb
makes	verb
a	indefinite article
delicious	adjective
cake	noun (direct object)
in	preposition
the	definite article
kitchen	noun

- The definite article is the grammatical name given to the word 'the'.
- The indefinite article is the name given to the word 'a' or 'an'.
- A noun is a person, place, thing or animal (e.g. Tom, London, chair, cat).
- A verb is a word that describes an action (e.g. eats, slept, is going).
- An adjective is a word that describes a noun (e.g. pretty, old, blue).
- An adverb is a word that describes a verb. It tells you how an action is done (e.g. quickly, nicely, easily). Many adverbs in English end in '-ly'.
- A preposition is a word placed before a noun or a pronoun to indicate time, place or condition (e.g. on the table).
- A conjunction is a word that links two parts of a sentence (e.g. 'He was eating and drinking'). The most common conjunctions in English are 'and' and 'but'.
- A pronoun is a word that stands in place of a noun. In the sentence on the previous page, we could replace the noun 'the girl' by the pronoun 'she'. Similarly, 'a cake' could be replaced by 'it'.
- A relative pronoun is a word that links one part of a sentence to another. In English the relative pronouns are 'who', 'whom', 'which', 'where' and 'that', e.g. 'I gave him all the money that I earned'. The two parts of the sentence – 'I gave him all the money' and 'I earned' – are linked together by the relative pronoun 'that'.
- A negative is a word like 'not' or 'never' that indicates an action is not being done.
- Gender refers to whether a word is masculine or feminine.
- The subject is the name given to the person or thing doing the action. In the sentence on the previous page, the subject is 'the girl'.
- The direct object is the name given to the person or thing that has the action done directly to it. In the sentence on the previous page, 'a cake' is the object because it is made by the girl.

PROGRESS CHECK

1. Read this sentence and answer the following questions:
   The clumsy goalkeeper suddenly dropped the ball.
   (a) What is the subject?
   (b) Find the verb.
   (c) Find an adjective.
   (d) Find an adverb.
   (e) Find a definite article.

2. Read this sentence and answer the following questions:
   He dropped it at my feet and I scored.
   (a) Find an object pronoun.
   (b) Find a preposition.
   (c) Find a noun.
   (d) Find a conjunction.

2. (a) it
(b) at
(c) feet
(d) and

1. (a) goalkeeper
(b) dropped
(c) clumsy
(d) suddenly
(e) the

Definite and indefinite articles

AQA	✓
OCR	✓
EDEXCEL	✓
WJEC	✓
CCEA	✓

The definite article is the grammatical way of referring to 'the'. The indefinite article is the grammatical way of referring to 'a' or 'an'.

	Definite article (the)		Indefinite article (a, an, some)	
	Masculine	Feminine	Masculine	Feminine
Singular	**el**	**la**	**un**	**una**
Plural	**los**	**las**	**unos**	**unas**

> **KEY POINT**
>
> **de + el** becomes **del**
> **a + el** becomes **al**
> e.g. **el libro del niño**   the boy's book
>   **Fui al supermercado.**   I went to the supermarket.

El and **un** are also used before feminine nouns that begin with a stressed **a-** or **ha-** (but not when separated by an adjective).

el agua	the water
el arma	the weapon
la vieja arma	the old weapon
But **la alfombra**	the carpet (the **a-** is not stressed)

However, the gender of the noun does not actually change, so all other changes are the same as for other feminine nouns…

El agua está fría.   The water is cold.

… and the plural is always **las** or **unas**.

las aguas	the waters
las armas	the weapons
unas armas	some weapons

The definite article is used…

- when referring to nouns in a general sense:
  El vino es importante en España.   Wine is important in Spain.

- with the name of a language, except when it comes directly after **aprender**, **hablar** or **saber**:
  El español es fácil.   Spanish is easy.
  Hablo español.   I speak Spanish.

- before titles:
  la reina Isabel   Queen Elizabeth
  el señor García   Mr García

> **KEY POINT**
>
> You leave out the article when talking directly to the person:
> **Buenos días, Señor García.**   Good morning, Mr García.

- when saying 'on Saturday', 'on Friday', etc.:

el sábado	on Saturday
el viernes	on Friday
los sábados	on Saturdays

- in certain expressions when it is not used in English:

en la cama	in bed
en el hospital	in hospital
en la iglesia	in church
en la televisión	on television
en la cárcel	in prison
en el colegio	at school

The indefinite article is omitted…

- before occupations and nationalities:

Ella es profesora.	She is a teacher.
Él es inglés.	He is an Englishman.

- before **medio**, **mil**, **¡qué… !** and **tal**:

medio litro	half a litre
mil euros	a thousand euros
¡Qué día!	What a day!
tal cosa	such a thing

Nouns

AQA	✓
OCR	✓
EDEXCEL	✓
WJEC	✓
CCEA	✓

Unusual genders

The following nouns end in -a, but are masculine.

el problema	problem	**el futbolista**	footballer
el programa	programme	**el clima**	climate
el síntoma	symptom	**el día**	day
el sistema	system	**el idioma**	language
el mapa	map	**el tema**	theme
el pijama	pyjamas	**el drama**	drama

The following nouns end in -o, but are feminine.

la foto	photograph	**la moto**	motorcycle
la mano	hand	**la radio**	radio

Compound nouns are masculine.

el abrelatas	tin-opener	**el parabrisas**	windscreen
el sacacorchos	corkscrew	**el lavaplatos**	dishwasher

Some words can be both masculine and feminine, but they change their meaning according to their gender.

el cura	priest	**la cura**	cure
el pendiente	earring	**la pendiente**	slope
el policía	policeman	**la policía**	police

Plurals

To form the plural of nouns, add -s to an unstressed vowel and -es to a consonant.			
el chico	boy	**los chicos**	boys
el dolor	pain	**los dolores**	pains
la silla	chair	**las sillas**	chairs
la flor	flower	**las flores**	flowers

Words ending in -z change the -z to -ces in the plural.			
el lápiz	pencil	**los lápices**	pencils
la vez	time	**las veces**	times

Words ending in a stressed -ión, -ón or -és lose their accents in the plural.			
la canción	song	**las canciones**	songs
el francés	Frenchman	**los franceses**	the French
el montón	pile	**los montones**	piles

KEY POINT

Note that the following usually denote a mixture of sexes:

los abuelos (grandparents)

los hermanos (brothers and sisters)

los hijos (children, i.e. boys and girls)

PROGRESS CHECK

Say or write the following in Spanish:

1. The teacher's chair
2. I went to the market.
3. The new carpet
4. The dirty water
5. The water is dirty.
6. English is easy.
7. I speak English.
8. King Charles
9. Good evening, Mr Gómez.
10. I went there on Saturday.

1. La silla del profesor/de la profesora   2. Fui al mercado.   3. La alfombra nueva   4. El agua sucia   5. El agua está sucia.   6. El inglés es fácil.   7. Hablo inglés.   8. El rey Carlos   9. Buenas tardes, Señor Gómez.   10. Fui allí el sábado.

Sample controlled assessment

Speaking

1 You are going to have a conversation with your teacher about the pictures below.

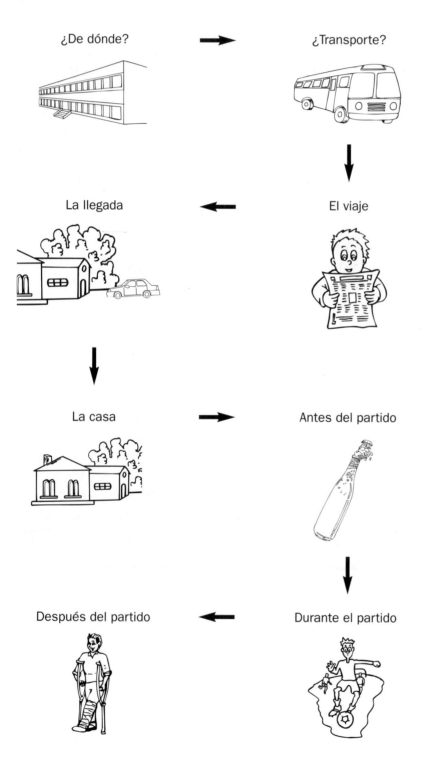

¿De dónde? → ¿Transporte?

La llegada ← El viaje

La casa → Antes del partido

Después del partido ← Durante el partido

Examiner's comments

Your teacher can choose any title or format for your controlled speaking assessment. Your teacher might give you a series of pictures to describe, such as the ones opposite about a football trip to Spain that did not go quite to plan. A model conversation is given on page 25.

Your controlled speaking assessment will last between four and six minutes. That is a long time. It means you will have to give plenty of detail to fill the time.

Sample controlled assessment

Student: Acabo de[20] volver de una visita inolvidable[15] a España. Mi instituto juega un partido anualmente contra un instituto español desde hace[26] años. La gran aventura empezó hace tres semanas.[16] Todo el equipo se encontró[11] muy de mañana[16] delante del instituto y nos marchamos a España a las seis de la mañana en autocar y después de un viaje largo de 24 horas llegamos a la entrada del instituto español. Nuestras familias anfitrionas nos[32] esperaban.

Teacher: ¿Qué hiciste durante el viaje?

Student: Durante el viaje, leía y escuchaba música. Al llegar,[7] en seguida, sin perder un momento[5] fuimos a casa de Pedro en coche. Su padre conducía. Su casa era pequeña pero confortable. Había un pequeño[15] jardín encantador con flores y césped, pero los jardines británicos son los mejores del mundo.[23]

Teacher: ¿Tenías hambre?

Student: No. No tenía ganas[1] de comer. Después de dormir[8] un poco, salí a entrenarme. Hicimos ejercicio y jugamos con el balón. Luego volvimos a casa y pasé la tarde viendo la tele y charlando con mi familia anfitriona. Más tarde, fuimos a un bar a beber algo y a charlar con nuestros amigos españoles. El ambiente era estupendo.

Teacher: Y ¿al día siguiente?

Student: Al día siguiente, mi amigo español se reunió con sus amigos. Hacía buen tiempo y el sol brillaba. A pesar del[19] calor, a las tres de la tarde, el partido empezó. Al final de la primera parte ganábamos 2-0 y yo había metido[17] uno de los goles de tiro libre. Pero justo después del descanso ¡Qué desastre![9] Me hice daño.

Teacher: ¿Qué pasó?

Student: Uno de los jugadores españoles se enfadó porque[2] su equipo perdía.[13] Su entrada fue muy violenta. Me rompió la pierna. El dolor era increíble. Mis compañeros no estaban contentos tampoco.[24] Mi profe llamó a una ambulancia y llegó diez minutos más tarde. Me quedé tres días en el hospital y mis amigos vinieron a verme todos los días. El hospital era agradable y las enfermeras me[32] cuidaron bien.

Teacher: ¿Tus amigos llevaron regalos?

Student: Sí, me dieron fruta, chocolate y libros. El equipo español vino a verme. El jugador violento me pidió perdón. Me dio un reloj de oro de regalo. Sus padres escribieron a mis padres para pedir[31] perdón. Creo que mi visita a España fue un desastre[3] y no volveré nunca.[24] Esperemos[25] que no. No sería[14] una buena idea.

Turn to page 155 for a translation of this passage.

Examiner's comments

This student has used most of the '32 points for improving your grade' from pages 8–9 and is on track for a top grade:

1. A 'tener' structure
2. Use of 'porque'
3. A justified point of view
5. 'Sin' + the infinitive
7. 'Al' + the infinitive
8. 'Después de' + the infinitive
9. An exclamation
11. A reflexive preterite
13. An example of the imperfect
14. A conditional has been used
15. Two examples of adjectives in this passage
16. Impressive vocabulary and structures, e.g. 'hace tres semanas'
17. A pluperfect has been included
19. 'A pesar de'
20. 'Acabar de'
23. A superlative has been used
24. Two examples of the negative
25. An example of the subjunctive. Very impressive!
26. A 'desde hace' structure
31. 'Para' + the infinitive
32. Pronouns have been used

Sample controlled assessment

Writing

1. Write an imaginary magazine interview with a Spanish-speaking celebrity tennis player, addressing the following points:

   - Introduce the person to the reader
   - Keeping fit
   - His/her early career
   - Leisure interests
   - His/her family
   - Views on the world today.

Interview con Isabel Fretey - estrella internacional.
Todo el mundo ha oído hablar de Isabel: la mejor tenista[23] de España.
Ya a la edad de 24 años había ganado[17] tres torneos y este verano
va[12] a intentar ganar el torneo de Wimbledon. Madrileña, guapa, es
una verdadera estrella. Pero su vida no siempre ha sido fácil.

Isabel, cuéntame unos detalles de tu juventud.
La vida era dura. ¡Qué pesadilla![9] Mis padres murieron cuando tenía[13]
tres años y fui a vivir con mi tía en un barrio conflictivo de Madrid. No
había instalaciones para jugar a tenis. Para jugar,[31] tenía que coger el
metro y viajar una hora. Finalmente encontré un buen club. Era
miembro desde hace[26] un año cuando conocí a Marcel quien es ahora
mi entrenador y mi marido.

Y ¿qué haces para mantenerte en forma?
Lo importante es[16] comer bien. Nunca bebo alcohol,[24] no fumo y
hago ejercicio. Y juego al tenis cuatro horas al día con Marcel.

Y ¿tu primer triunfo?
Gané mi primer torneo en los Estados Unidos. Estaba tan contenta.
Después de ganar,[8] celebré la victoria en un restaurante de cinco estrellas.

Además del tenis, ¿qué te gusta hacer?
Me encanta la lectura. Al volver[7] a casa, lo que me gusta es sentarme
en una butaca y leer una novela.

Y ¿tu familia?
Soy hija única y mi tía está muerta. Pero tengo Marcel, mi marido, y
un día espero tener hijos. Pero antes de[6] tener hijos, tengo ganas de[1]
ganar más torneos. Es importante que vaya[25] a Wimbledon y tengo que
ganar.

Y ¿los problemas del mundo?
En mi opinión, el problema principal[15] es el medio ambiente. La gente
no hace caso a lo que pasa. Estamos destruyendo el planeta.[3]

Isabel, suerte en Wimbledon.
Gracias.

Turn to page 155 for a translation of this passage.

Examiner's comments

Remember that you will have to write two controlled assessments, each of up to 300 words. Here is a good example that uses a number of the '32 points for improving your grade' from pages 8–9:

1 A 'tener' structure
3 A justified point of view
6 'Antes de...'
7 'Al' + the infinitive
8 'Después de' + the infinitive
9 An exclamation
12 The future tense has been used
13 The imperfect tense has been used
15 One example of an adjective
16 An impressive structure
17 An example of the pluperfect
23 An example of the superlative
24 A negative has been used
25 A subjunctive. Superb!
26 A 'desde hace' structure
31 'Para' + the infinitive

Exam practice questions

Listening

 What are these people going to have to eat and drink? Write the correct letters in the answer spaces provided.

A

B

C

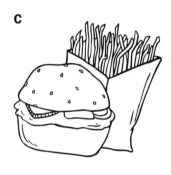

D

E

F

(a) ....

(b) ....

(c) ....

(d) ....

(4)

2 Track 4 You hear this conversation in a restaurant.

(a) What does the waiter ask? ....

(b) Where is the table? ....

(c) What will the waiter bring? ....

(d) What does he recommend? ....

(e) What is in the omelette? ....

(f) What does the customer want as a starter? ....

(g) What does the customer want as a dessert? ....

(h) What does the customer want to drink? ....

(8)

Exam practice questions

3 Track 5 You are in a café. What do the five customers ask for? Write the correct letters in the answer spaces provided.

To eat

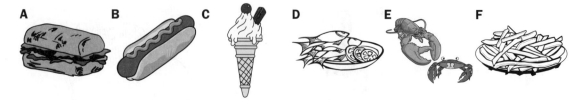

A   B   C   D   E   F

To drink

A   B   C   D   E   F

(a)	Customer 1:	**(i)** To eat	**(ii)** To drink	
(b)	Customer 2:	**(i)** To eat	**(ii)** To drink	
(c)	Customer 3:	**(i)** To eat	**(ii)** To drink	
(d)	Customer 4:	**(i)** To eat	**(ii)** To drink	
(e)	Customer 5:	**(i)** To eat	**(ii)** To drink	**(10)**

4 Track 6 You are ill and go to see the doctor. What caused your illness? Tick the two correct boxes.

A   **B**

☐   ☐

C   **D**

☐   ☐   **(2)**

Exam practice questions

5 **Track 7** Isabel and Antonio are talking about smoking. Tick the correct boxes.

		True	False
(a)	Antonio does not smoke because of the smell.	☐	☐
(b)	Antonio's girlfriend smokes.	☐	☐
(c)	Isabel started smoking when she was 15.	☐	☐
(d)	Isabel smoked because her friends did.	☐	☐
(e)	Isabel smokes very little.	☐	☐
(f)	Isabel wants to stop smoking.	☐	☐
(g)	Isabel's parents are smokers.	☐	☐
(h)	Isabel's parents do not want her to smoke.	☐	☐
(i)	Isabel smokes at home.	☐	☐
(j)	Isabel earns money by working.	☐	☐
(k)	Isabel drinks wine occasionally.	☐	☐

(11)

6 **Track 8** At the grocer's. What do they buy? There are two sections.

Section 1:

Put a cross in the correct boxes.

	Pears	Apples	Grapes	Bananas
The man				

	Ham	Sausages	Eggs	Milk
The woman				

Section 2:

Put a cross in the correct boxes.

	Water	Bread	Cheese	Sweets
The man				

	Flowers	Cereal	Cooking oil	Wine
The woman				

(8)

WJEC Foundation Tier

Exam practice questions

Reading

1 You see this sign.

> BUSCAMOS A ESTE HOMBRE.
> POR ASESINATO.
> POR SECUESTRO DE UN NIÑO.
> POR ATRACO A UNA JOYERÍA.
> SE LLAMA JORGE PÉREZ.
> ES PERUANO. TIENE CUARENTA AÑOS.
> HA PASADO VEINTE AÑOS EN LA CÁRCEL.
> SE ESCAPÓ DE LA CÁRCEL HACE UNA SEMANA.
> ES ALTO, DELGADO, NO LLEVA GAFAS, TIENE BIGOTE.

(a) Which crimes has Jorge committed? Tick the three correct boxes.

   A He robbed a bank ☐

   B He committed fraud ☐

   C He kidnapped someone ☐

   D He stole diamonds, gold, etc. ☐

   E He killed someone ☐

   F He wounded a policeman ☐ **(3)**

(b) Where is he from?

   A South America ☐   **B** Australia ☐   **C** Europe ☐   **D** Africa ☐ **(1)**

(c) How old is he?

   A 18 ☐   **B** 20 ☐   **C** 30 ☐   **D** 40 ☐ **(1)**

(d) Where was he a week ago?

   A In prison ☐   **B** In a bank ☐   **C** In Peru ☐   **D** In a jeweller's ☐ **(1)**

(e) Which one is Jorge?

   A   **B**   **C**   **D**

(1)

Exam practice questions

2 Read the advert below, then answer the questions that follow.

> ### Restaurant Tulipán
>
> *El restaurante Tulipán es el restaurante más caro de la ciudad. Pero ofrece una gama de platos que contribuye a mantener una dieta equilibrada. Además, presta una especial atención a la calidad de todos los productos que ofrecemos. Aquí sabemos lo que te gusta.*

(a) What makes the restaurant stand out from others in the city?

....

(b) How does the restaurant's choice of dishes help you?

....

(c) To what do they pay special attention at the restaurant?

....

(d) What do they claim to know at the restaurant?

.... **(4)**

3 A friend sends you this e-mail.

> Ayer, volvía de la casa de mi amiga en el centro de la ciudad cuando vi un accidente. Hacía muy mal tiempo. Llovía a chorros y hacía frío. Una bicicleta se acercaba a un cruce y un camión chocó con la bicicleta. El ciclista se cayó y el camión paró. Sin perder un momento fui a atender al ciclista. Tenía el brazo roto pero podía hablar. Había sangre por todas partes. Saqué mi móbil y llamé a los ambulancieros. Afortunadamente llegaron cinco minutos más tarde y se llevaron al herido al hospital. Luego un policía me hizo muchas preguntas sobre el accidente y tuve que ir a la comisaría para escribir lo que había visto. Esta mañana el ciclista me llamó para darme las gracias por lo que había hecho. Juan

(a) Where was Juan returning from? .... **(1)**

(b) Give three details about the weather.

    (i) ....

    (ii) ....

    (iii) .... **(3)**

(c) What collided with the bicycle? .... **(1)**

(d) What injury did the cyclist have? .... **(1)**

(e) What did Juan take out? .... **(1)**

(f) Where did Juan go after the accident? .... **(1)**

(g) Why did the cyclist phone Juan? .... **(1)**

Exam practice questions

4 Read the article below, then answer the questions that follow.

> ## Un triunfo español
> Una de las comidas típicas de España es la tortilla de patatas. Es deliciosa – los ingredientes son huevos, patatas y cebollas. La tortilla se come a cualquier hora en España. Se come como plato principal con carne o pescado o con ensalada. Y ¿tres trucos para una tortilla excelente? Hay que freír las cebollas lentamente. Los huevos deben ser huevos de granja y debes batir los huevos un máximo de 30 segundos. En Inglaterra las tortillas son asquerosas porque los ingleses las preparan demasiado de prisa y les falta sabor.

(a) When do Spaniards eat omelettes? .... **(1)**

(b) What three things can you eat with omelettes?

.... **(3)**

(c) What three three tips are given for making a good omelette?

    (i) ....

    (ii) ....

    (iii) .... **(3)**

(d) According to the article, why do omelettes in England lack flavour?

.... **(1)**

5 Read the article below, then answer the questions that follow.

> El 'picnic' es una idea británica. Para los ingleses, es la solución ideal para que la gente disfrute de la naturaleza y los días de sol. Pero hay que comer bien y de una manera sana. Se deben comer platos de poca grasa, por ejemplo pollo, atún, salmón o verduras. Para el postre, la solución más sana es la fruta pero hay que tener mucho cuidado si las llevas en mochila. Debes elegir las que son resistentes a los golpes: naranjas, manzanas. Para conservar los alimentos en perfectas condiciones, lleva una nevera pequeña.

(a) Where did the idea of a picnic come from? .... **(1)**

(b) Name two things that a picnic lets you enjoy.

    (i) ....   **(ii)** .... **(2)**

(c) What advice is given about the choice of food? .... **(1)**

(d) Name four things that have low fat.

    (i) ....   **(ii)** ....

    (iii) ....   **(iv)** .... **(4)**

(e) What should be eaten for dessert? .... **(1)**

(f) What quality do apples and oranges have? .... **(1)**

(g) What would keep the food in good condition? .... **(1)**

2 Relationships and choices

The following topics are covered in this chapter:

- Relationships with family and friends
- Future plans regarding marriage or partnership
- Social issues
- Equality
- Grammar

2.1 Relationships with family and friends

LEARNING SUMMARY	After studying this section, you should be able to: • talk about your family, friends and pets • describe your relationships with people

Relationships with family and friends

AQA	✓
OCR	✓
EDEXCEL	✓
WJEC	✓
CCEA	✓

You will find the following vocabulary and sentences useful for the listening and reading exams. You might carry out a controlled assessment on relationships with family and friends in either speaking or writing.

Family

el papá — la abuela

la mamá — el abuelo

la hermana — el hermano

Self and family (Mi familia y yo)

el/la abuelo/a – grandfather/grandmother

el amo/la ama de casa – house husband/wife

el/la bebé – baby

la boda – wedding, marriage

la cohabitación – living together

el/la cuñado/a – brother-in-law/ sister-in-law

la disputa – argument

el divorcio – divorce

embarazada – pregnant

el/la esposo/a – husband/wife

la familia – family

la familia monoparental – single-parent family

los familiares – relations

el/la gemelo/a – twin

el/la hermano/a – brother/sister

el/la hijo/a – son/daughter

el hogar – home

la madre – mother

la mamá – mum

el marido – husband

la mujer – wife

el/la nieto/a – grandson/ granddaughter

el/la niño/a – child

el/la novio/a – boyfriend/girlfriend

el padre – father

el padre/la madre soltero/a – single parent

los padres – parents

el papá – dad

la pareja – partner

el/la pariente – relation

el/la primo/a – cousin

las relaciones – relationship

la separación – separation

el/la sobrino/a – nephew/niece

el/la suegro/a – father-in-law/ mother-in-law

el/la tío/a – uncle/aunt

el/la viudo/a – widower/widow

embarazada

KEY POINT

Notice that **pariente** means 'relation', not 'parent'.

Friends and personal contacts (Los amigos y los contactos personales)

el abrazo – embrace, hug

la amistad – friendship

el amor – love

el beso – kiss

la bienvenida – welcome

la broma – joke

el carácter – character

el cariño – affection

la carta – letter

el chiste – joke

la cita – date (i.e. to meet a friend)

la conversación – conversation

la correspondencia – correspondence

la culpa – blame

los demás – the rest

el deseo – desire

el diálogo – conversation

el favor – favour

el gusto – pleasure

el humor – humour

la invitación – invitation

la pelea – fight

la postal – postcard

la promesa – promise

la señal – sign, signal

la sonrisa – smile

la tarjeta – card

la visita – visit

el beso

Verbs

dar la mano

acompañar – to accompany	**llevarse bien con** – to get on well with
acordarse – to remember	**llevarse mal con** – to get on badly with
ayudar – to help	**llorar** – to cry
besar – to kiss	**morir** – to die
celebrar – to celebrate	**nacer** – to be born
charlar – to chat	**odiar** – to hate
conocer – to know	**parecer** – to seem
contar – to tell, to count	**pedir un favor** – to ask a favour
convivir, cohabitar – to live together	**preferir** – to prefer
crecer – to grow	**presentar** – to introduce
cumplir – to reach (a birthday)	**prometer** – to promise
dar la mano – to shake hands	**querer** – to love, to want
dar las gracias – to thank	**recoger** – to pick up
detestar – to hate	**reconocer** – to recognise
divorciarse – to get divorced	**recordar** – to remember
echar de menos – to miss (i.e. a person)	**regalar** – to give a present
echar una carta – to post a letter	**reír(se)** – to laugh
elegir – to choose	**salir** – to go out
enamorarse – to fall in love	**saludar** – to greet
encantar – to delight	**separarse** – to separate
enfadarse – to get angry	**sonreír(se)** – to smile
evitar – to avoid	**tutear** – to use 'tú'
invitar – to invite	**ver** – to see
llamarse – to be called	**visitar** – to visit
	volver a casarse – to re-marry

Pets (Los animales)

el loro

la cobaya – guinea pig	**los peces tropicales** – tropical fish
el conejo – rabbit	**el periquito** – parakeet, budgie
el gato – cat	**el perro** – dog
el hámster – hamster	**el pez** – fish
el insecto palo – stick insect	**el pez de colores** – goldfish
la jaula – cage	**el ratón** – mouse
el loro – parrot	**la tortuga** – tortoise

People (La gente)

el adolescente

el/la adolescente – adolescent, teenager	**el/la enemigo/a** – enemy
el/la adulto/a – adult	**el hombre** – man
el/la amigo/a – friend	**el huésped** – guest
el caballero – gentleman	**el/la invitado/a** – guest
el/la chico/chica – boy/girl	**el/la muchacho/a** – boy/girl
el/la compañero/a – friend	**la pareja** – couple
el/la amigo/a por correo – penfriend	**la persona** – person
el desconocido – stranger	**todo el mundo** – everybody
	el/la vecino/a – neighbour

PROGRESS CHECK

Say or write the following in Spanish:

1 Grandfather
2 To go out
3 Gentleman
4 Tortoise
5 I have a cat and a goldfish.
6 I have a nephew and two nieces.
7 I went to the shops with my family.

1. El abuelo   2. Salir   3. El caballero   4. La tortuga   5. Tengo un gato y un pez de colores.
6. Tengo un sobrino y dos sobrinas.   7. Fui a las tiendas con mi familia.

Conversation: Grades G–D

AQA ✓
OCR ✓
EDEXCEL ✓
WJEC ✓
CCEA ✓

Make sure you can answer these questions without thinking. Get someone to ask you these questions so you can practise answering them without using the book.

¿Cómo te llamas?
Me llamo … .

¿Cuántos años tienes?
Tengo … años.

¿Cuántos sois en tu familia?
Somos … .

¿Quiénes son?
Son mi padre, mi madre, mi hermano y yo.

¿En qué trabaja tu padre?
Es profesor.

¿En qué trabaja tu madre?
Es … .

¿En qué año naciste?
Nací en mil novecientos noventa y tres.

¿Cuánto mides?
Mido un metro ochenta.

¿Tienes animales en casa?
Tengo un perro/un gato.

¿Cuándo es tu cumpleaños?
Es el veintisiete de septiembre.

KEY POINT

- Note that in Spanish you do not say **un** when stating someone's job. For example, you have to say **es profesor** (he is teacher).
- **Medir** means 'to measure'; **¿Cuánto mides?** = How tall are you?

Conversation: Grades C–A*

AQA	✓
OCR	✓
EDEXCEL	✓
WJEC	✓
CCEA	✓

You will be assessed on your communication skills and also on your quality of language. Follow these tips when preparing for the controlled speaking assessment:

- Try to use impressive vocabulary: make your own personal list of out-of-the-ordinary words.
- Try to put expression into what you say.
- Your answers should not be a pre-learnt speech.
- Why not record your answers and listen to them whenever you can?[1]

1 Show your knowledge of tenses. You are unlikely to get a grade C unless you know your tenses.

2 It is important to give as much information as you can.

Describe a tu familia.

En mi familia somos cuatro: mi madre, mi padre, mi hermana y yo. Tenemos también un perro. Mi padre trabaja en una oficina. No sé exactamente lo que hace. Mi madre es dentista.[2]

¿Cómo es tu padre?

Mi padre es grande y tiene los ojos negros. Tiene cuarenta y cinco años y le gusta leer periódicos y ver la televisión.

¿Cómo es tu madre?

Mi madre es pequeña y bonita. Tiene los ojos marrones y el pelo largo y negro. Tiene cuarenta y dos años y le gusta trabajar en el jardín y salir con mi padre.

¿Cómo es tu hermana?

Mi hermana tiene treinta años y es muy simpática. Tiene los ojos azules, el pelo largo y rubio y lleva gafas. Le gusta la música pop y ver la televisión.

¿Tienes otros parientes?

Sí, tengo otros parientes, muchos sobrinos, muchos tíos, muchos primos. Mis abuelos nos visitan a menudo.

¿Cuál es el animal que te gusta más?

Me gustan los perros porque son muy cariñosos y limpios.[3]

El día de tu cumpleaños, ¿qué regalos recibiste?[4]

Recibí ropa, CDs y dinero.

¿Qué hiciste con el dinero?[5]

Compré más ropa, salí con mis amigos e ingresé[6] el resto en el banco.

¿Qué vas a hacer con el dinero del banco?[7]

Compraré regalos para mi familia e[8] iré de vacaciones.

3 You have given an opinion and justified it. This gives you extra marks.

4 A chance to use a preterite (see pages 93–94).

5 Another chance to use preterites.

6 Only three preterites?

7 A chance to use the future (see pages 123–124).

8 It is wrong to say 'y iré'. 'Y' changes to 'e' before a word beginning with 'i'.

Other useful sentences

La vida familiar en Gran Bretaña.
Family life in Great Britain.

Cada día en Gran Bretaña se casan 800 parejas, se divorcian 300 parejas y nacen 3000 niños.
Every day in Great Britain 800 couples get married, 300 couples get divorced and 3000 children are born.

El número de personas solteras crece.
The number of single people is increasing.

Aumenta el número de solteros, jubilados, divorciados y viudos que viven solos.
The number of single, retired, divorced and widowed people who live alone is increasing.

Según un sondeo reciente...
In a recent survey...

Muchos niños son testigos del divorcio y de las posteriores relaciones de sus padres.

A lot of children see their parents separating and then new friendships beginning.

Muchos niños viven con hermanastros y hermanastras.

A lot of children live with half-brothers and half-sisters.

Mis relaciones con mis padres son excelentes/buenas/malas.

I have an excellent/good/bad relationship with my parents.

> **KEY POINT**
>
> Note that **relaciones** in the sentence above means 'relationship'.

Si tengo un problema, lo discuto con mis amigos, no con mis padres.

If I have a problem, I discuss it with my friends, not with my parents.

A mi edad, amigos son más importantes que mi familia.

At my age, friends are more important than my family.

A mi edad, quiero llevar la ropa que escojo yo.

At my age, I want to wear the clothes that I choose.

Está mimada.

She is spoilt.

Tener un hermano mayor es un problema.

Having an older brother is a problem.

Me llevo bien con mis padres.

I get on well with my parents.

No me llevo bien con mi hermano.

I do not get on with my brother.

> **KEY POINT**
>
> **Llevarse bien** means 'to get on well with'.

En una familia numerosa nunca estás solo y eso me gusta.

In a large family you are never alone and I like that.

En una familia numerosa nunca estás solo y eso no me gusta porque no tienes una vida privada y hay demasiado ruido.

In a large family you are never alone and I do not like it because you have no private life and there is too much noise.

Hay ventajas y desventajas.

There are advantages and disadvantages.

Si eres hijo único/hija única, te sientes solo/sola.

If you are an only child, you feel alone.

Mis padres no quieren escuchar mi punto de vista.

My parents do not want to hear my point of view.

Si tienes un problema, puedes contar con tu familia.

If you have a problem, you can rely on your family.

> **KEY POINT**
>
> **Contar con** means 'to rely on'.

Quiero recibir una cantidad fija de dinero de bolsillo.

I would like to get a set amount of pocket money.

Mis padres se preocupan demasiado.

My parents worry too much.

Mis padres quieren saber con quién salgo, adónde voy y a qué hora vuelvo a casa.

My parents want to know who I go out with, where I am going and what time I will get home.

El sida, las drogas, el alcohol, las violaciones – hay muchos peligros para los jóvenes.

Aids, drugs, alcohol, rape – there are a lot of dangers facing young people.

Mis padres se separaron y vivo con...

My parents separated and I live with...

Rara vez comemos juntos.

We rarely eat together.

Las chicas tienen menos libertad que los chicos.

Girls have less freedom than boys.

Mis padres no me cuidan bien.

My parents do not look after me well.

En mi familia, (no) nos entendemos bien.

In my family, we (do not) get on with each other.

Es muy simpático/a, servicial, duro/a, pesado/a, esnob.

He/she is very nice/helpful/harsh/annoying/snobby.

El padre ideal no existe.

The ideal parent does not exist.

Nunca miente.

He/she never lies.

> **KEY POINT**
>
> **Mentir** means 'to lie'.

Las apariencias engañan.

Appearances are deceptive.

No puedo salir con chicos.

I cannot go out with boys.

triste

Describing people (Describiendo a la gente)

agresivo/a – aggressive
antipático/a – nasty
arrogante – arrogant
callado/a – quiet

cortés – polite
hablador(a) – talkative
honesto/a – honest
ruidoso/a – noisy

sensato/a – sensible
tímido/a – shy
triste – sad

PROGRESS CHECK

Say or write the following in Spanish:
1. In a recent survey
2. I have an excellent relationship with my parents.
3. She is spoilt.
4. There are advantages and disadvantages.
5. My parents worry too much.

5. Mis padres se preocupan demasiado.
4. Hay ventajas y desventajas.
3. Está mimada.
2. Tengo relaciones excelentes con mis padres.
1. Según un sondeo reciente

2.2 Future plans regarding marriage or partnership

LEARNING SUMMARY	**After studying this section, you should be able to:**
	• explain your plans or other people's plans for marriage or partnership
	• give views on marriage and parenthood

Marriage and partnership

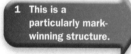

AQA	✓
OCR	✓
EDEXCEL	✓
WJEC	✓
CCEA	✓

These sentences contain vocabulary and structures that will help you in the listening and reading exams, and in the controlled assessment.

Voy a describir mi futuro.

I am going to describe my future.

No voy a casarme antes de la edad de 30 años y tendré tres niños.

I won't get married until I am 30 and will have three children.

Me casaré a la edad de 24 años.

I will get married when I am 24.

Estaré contento/a porque llevaré mi vida a mi manera.

I will be happy because I will lead my life in my own way.

> **KEY POINT**
>
> Note that **llevar una vida** means 'to lead a life'.

Vivire en una casa de lujo pero no quiero casarme.

I will have a luxury house but I will not get married.

Cuando termine el colegio...[1]

When I leave school...

Cuando haya terminado mis estudios...[1]

When I have finished my studies...

> **1** This is a particularly mark-winning structure.

> **KEY POINT**
>
> The Spanish use a subjunctive after **cuando** when a future time frame is following.

Espero encontrar a una pareja simpática.

I hope to find a nice partner.

Voy a casarme con una persona famosa.

I will marry a celebrity.

En un futuro seré feliz en la vida.

Later in life I am going to be happy.

Seré amo/ama de casa.

I will be a house husband/wife.

Mi pareja seguirá trabajando y yo me quedaré en casa.

My partner will carry on working and I will stay at home.

Note how to say 'to carry on (doing something)' = **seguir** + present participle.

Yo cuidaré de los niños en casa.
I will look after the children at home.

Cuidar is 'to look after', **buscar** is 'to look for' and **mirar** is 'to look at'.

El matrimonio (no) es importante para una buena relación.
Marriage is (not) important for a good relationship.

Es un vínculo que une la pareja.
It is a bond that unites the couple.

Unir means 'to unite'.

Voy a casarme porque es importante que los niños tengan estabilidad.
I am going to get married because stability is important for children.

No entiendo por qué la gente no quiere casarse.
I do not understand why people do not want to get married.

Es más sencillo cohabitar sin casarse.
It is simpler to live together without getting married.

No quiero niños.
I do not want children.

Lo de tener niños me da miedo.
I am frightened of having children.

Me encanta la idea de casarme.
I love the idea of getting married.

No estoy ni a favor ni en contra del matrimonio.
I am neither for nor against marriage.

Ser padre/madre forma parte de mis planes.
I plan to become a father/mother.

Será dentro de un año, de cinco años, ¡o quizás cuando tenga 60!
It will be in a year's time, or five years, or when I am 60!

Quiero niños, montones de niños.
I want children, loads of them!

Lo importante es el amor.
The important thing is love.

'Un montón' (plural 'montones' without the accent) really means 'a pile'. This is a colloquial way of saying 'lots' and will get you extra marks.

Say or write the following in Spanish:
1 I want to get married.
2 I do not want to get married.
3 I want to live with a partner.

3. Quiero vivir con una pareja.
2. No quiero casarme.
1. Quiero casarme.

2.3 Social issues

LEARNING SUMMARY

After studying this section, you should be able to:

- talk about homelessness, drugs, crime and smoking
- give views on social issues

Social issues

AQA	✓
OCR	✓
EDEXCEL	✗
WJEC	✓
CCEA	✓

You might like to do your speaking or writing controlled assessment on social issues. This topic might also appear on your listening and/or reading exam. You will find the following vocabulary and sentences invaluable.

Homelessness (Los sin techo)

la caja de cartón – cardboard box
dormir al raso – to sleep rough
fugarse de casa – to run away from home
la gente sin hogar/sin techo – homeless person
el/la mendigo/a – beggar

la necesidad de viviendas – housing needs
la pobreza – poverty
el refugio para los desamparados – shelter for the homeless
el vagabundo – tramp
vivir en la miseria – to live in poverty
vulnerable – vulnerable

> **KEY POINT**
>
> **Sin techo** literally means 'without a roof'.

En invierno, en los refugios reservan camas para los sin techo.
In winter, beds are kept for the homeless in shelters.
Pero en primavera, estas camas ya no están disponibles.
But in spring, these beds are no longer available.
Ciertos refugios tienen que cerrar por falta de dinero.
Some shelters close through lack of money.
Abandonó su hogar para ser mendigo en una ciudad.
He left the family home to be a beggar in a city.
Gana dinero vendiendo *The Big Issue*.
He earns money by selling *The Big Issue*.

> **KEY POINT**
>
> Use the present participle to say 'on (doing something)' or 'by (doing something)'.

Se encuentra en un círculo vicioso.
He is in a vicious circle.
En el Reino Unido hay 5000 personas sin techo.
In the UK there are 5000 homeless people.

> **KEY POINT**
>
> The UK means England, Scotland, Wales and Northern Ireland.

Se encuentra sin amigos y sin familia.
He has no friends or family.

Son ancianos, jóvenes, inmigrantes y madres con niños.
They are old people, young people, immigrants and mothers with children.

Viven al raso sin hogar.
They live in the open without any accommodation.

Algunos son enfermos mentales.
Some are mentally ill.

el criminal

Crime (El crimen)

amenazar – to threaten   **el/la criminal** – criminal   **el robo** – theft

armado/a – armed   **el ladrón** – thief, burglar   **el vandalismo** – vandalism

Tengo miedo cuando salgo.
I am frightened when I go out.

> **KEY POINT**
>
> **Tener miedo** literally means 'to have fear'.

En las escaleras y en cada esquina...
On the stairways and on every corner...

Hay grupos de gamberros.
There are groups of hooligans.

Te miran de forma amenazante.
They look at you menacingly.

Nos han robado.
We have been robbed.

La policía debería detenerlos.
The police should arrest them.

> **KEY POINT**
>
> Note that the conditional of **deber** means 'should'.

Vi un atraco en la ciudad.
I saw a hold-up in town.

Alguien llamó a la policía.
Someone told the police.

la jeringuilla

Drugs (La droga)

la adicción – addiction   **una droga dura** – hard drug   **la heroína** – heroin

el camello – drug peddler   **el/la drogadicto/a** – addict   **inyectarse** – to inject oneself

la cocaína – cocaine

desintoxicar – to detox   **drogarse** – to take drugs   **la jeringuilla** – syringe

una droga blanda – soft drug   **el éxtasis** – ecstasy   **la marihuana** – cannabis

En mi ciudad, la droga es un gran problema.
In my town, drugs are a big problem.

> **KEY POINT**
>
> Note that in Spanish they use the singular **la droga** and in English we use the plural 'drugs'.

Es la causa de mucho crimen.

It is the cause of a lot of crime.

Los drogadictos tienen que robar para poder comprar su dosis.

The drug addicts have to steal to be able to buy their fix.

Los jóvenes están tentados porque está prohibido y creen que drogarse es guay.

Young people are tempted because it is illegal and they think it is cool to take drugs.

Toman drogas por presión de grupo.

They take drugs because of peer group pressure.

No se saben las consecuencias a largo plazo.

The long term consequences are unknown.

fumar

Smoking (El tabaco)

atraer a los jóvenes – to attract young people

los fabricantes de cigarrillos – cigarette manufacturers

fumar – to smoke

fumar causa el cáncer – smoking causes cancer

fumar de forma pasiva – passive smoking

prohibir la publicidad – to prohibit advertising

el tabaquismo – addiction to smoking

Las última cifras dan miedo.

The latest figures are alarming.

> **KEY POINT**
>
> Note that **dar miedo** literally means 'to give fear'.

Ahora hay más chicas que chicos que fuman.

Now more girls than boys smoke.

Han prohibido los anuncios de tabaco.

They have forbidden cigarette advertising.

Tres chicas en diez fuman.

Three out of ten girls smoke.

Los fabricantes de cigarrillos intentan atraer a los jóvenes.

The cigarette manufacturers try to attract young people.

Las multinacionales animan a los jóvenes a fumar.

The multinationals encourage youngsters to smoke.

> **KEY POINT**
>
> Notice **animar** takes **a** before the next infinitive.

Distribuyen cigarrillos gratis en el tercer mundo para enganchar a los jóvenes.

They give out free cigarettes in the third world to hook young people.

El tabaco me calma los nervios.

Cigarettes calm my nerves.

Fuman para parecer mayores.

They smoke to look grown up.

Soy adicto/a al tabaco.

I am addicted to smoking.

Fumar de forma pasiva me preocupa.

Passive smoking worries me.

Hay gente que fuma para parecerse a sus amigos.

Some people smoke to be like their friends.

Son peligrosos para los pulmones.

They are dangerous for your lungs.

Dejé de fumar.

I stopped smoking.

> **KEY POINT**
>
> Note that **dejar** takes **de** before the next infinitive when it means 'to stop (doing something)'.

Es sociable.

It is sociable.

Ya no fumo.

I do not smoke anymore.

Antes fumaba regularmente.

I used to smoke regularly.

Han prohibido los anuncios de tabaco en la tele.

They have stopped cigarette advertising on TV.

Es muy malo para la salud.

It is very bad for your health.

Lo hacen para parecer sofisticados/as.

They smoke to look good.

> **KEY POINT**
>
> **Mirar** is 'to look', but when 'look' means 'seem' you should use the word **parecer**. **Aparecer** is 'appear' in the way ghosts do.

'Después de' with the infinitive is a good, mark-winning structure.

Después de ver una película sobre los peligros del tabaco...

After seeing a film about the dangers of smoking...

El tabaco contiene sustancias que son peligrosas para el corazón, la piel y sobre todo los pulmones.

Tobacco contains substances that are dangerous to the heart, the skin and most of all the lungs.

No tengo ganas de fumar más.

I do not want to smoke anymore.

> **KEY POINT**
>
> Another useful **tener** structure is demonstrated in the sentence above. **Tener ganas** really means 'to have a desire to'.

Nadie tiene derecho a hacer sufrir a los demás.

Nobody has the right to make others suffer.

Los fabricantes de cigarrillos financian la Fórmula uno.

Cigarette makers finance Formula 1.

Huele mal.

It stinks.

Mi ropa huele mal.

My clothes stink.

Tiene los dientes y los dedos amarillos.

He has yellow teeth and fingers.

Lo encuentra relajante y le libera del estrés.

He finds it relaxing and it gets rid of stress.

PROGRESS CHECK

Say or write the following in Spanish:

1. Passive smoking
2. We have been robbed.
3. There are too many homeless people.
4. He has yellow teeth and fingers.
5. It is very bad for your health.

1. Fumar de forma pasiva
2. Nos han robado.
3. Hay demasiadas personas sin hogar.
4. Tiene los dientes y los dedos amarillos.
5. Es muy malo para la salud.

2.4 Equality

LEARNING SUMMARY

After studying this section, you should be able to:

- talk about and give views on equality

Equality

AQA	✓
OCR	✗
EDEXCEL	✗
WJEC	✗
CCEA	✓

The following vocabulary and sentences will help you in the listening and reading exams, and in the controlled assessment.

Equality (La igualdad)

la igualdad de derechos – equal rights

la igualdad de oportunidades – equal opportunities

la igualdad entre sexos – sexual equality

los minusválidos – the disabled

la silla de ruedas – wheelchair

la situación de las mujeres – the position of women

Creo que es injusto.

I think that is unfair.

A igual trabajo, igual salario.

Equal pay for equal work.

Los minusválidos deben tener acceso a todo el edificio.

Disabed people must have access to the whole building.

El gobierno debe promover la igualdad de oportunidades.

The government must promote equal opportunities.

Las mujeres deben competir contra los hombres.

Women must compete with men.

Los hombres deben tratar a las mujeres como iguales.

Men must treat women as equals.

Es machista.

He is a chauvinist.

Es feminista.

She is a feminist.

Las chicas no pueden salir pero los chicos salen a cualquier hora.

Girls cannot go out but boys go out all the time.

Las chicas corren más riesgo que los chicos.

Girls are at greater risk than boys.

PROGRESS CHECK

Say or write the following in Spanish:

1. Equal opportunities
2. Chauvinist
3. As equals
4. Wheelchair

1. La igualdad de oportunidades
2. Machista
3. Como iguales
4. La silla de ruedas

2.5 Grammar

LEARNING SUMMARY	**After studying this section, you should be able to understand:**
	● the present tense

The present tense

AQA	✓
OCR	✓
EDEXCEL	✓
WJEC	✓
CCEA	✓

After studying this section, you should be familiar with the present tense in Spanish. Learn the regular verbs first, as they are the easiest. Unfortunately, most common Spanish verbs are irregular, and you just have to learn them individually.

KEY POINT

The infinitives of all verbs end in either **-ar**, **-er** or **-ir**.

Regular verbs

come

-ar verbs, e.g. mirar (to look)			
miro	I look	**miramos**	we look
miras	you (**tú**) look	**miráis**	you (**vosotros**) look
mira	he/she looks; you (**usted**) look	**miran**	they look; you (**ustedes**) look

-er verbs, e.g. comer (to eat)			
como	I eat	**comemos**	we eat
comes	you (**tú**) eat	**coméis**	you (**vosotros**) eat
come	he/she eats; you (**usted**) eat	**comen**	they eat; you (**ustedes**) eat

-ir verbs, e.g. vivir (to live)			
vivo	I live	**vivimos**	we live
vives	you (**tú**) live	**vivís**	you (**vosotros**) live
vive	he/she lives; you (**usted**) live	**viven**	they live; you (**ustedes**) live

PROGRESS CHECK

Say or write the following in Spanish:

1 I eat fish.
2 I look at Juan while he looks for his book.
3 They live in a city but I live in the country.

3. Viven en la ciudad pero yo vivo en el campo.
1. Como pescado.   2. Miro a Juan mientras busca su libro.

Radical-changing verbs

'Radical-changing' means that the stem of the verb changes when stressed.

KEY POINT

Because the endings are stressed in **nosotros** and **vosotros** forms, the stem does not change.

There are three groups of radical-changing verbs.

Group 1

Verbs that change **-e-** to **-ie-**. These can be **-ar**, **-er** or **-ir** verbs.

Group 1 -ar verbs			
cerrar to close			
cierro	I close	**cerramos**	we close
cierras	you close	**cerráis**	you close
cierra	he/she closes; you close	**cierran**	they close; you close
Verbs like **cerrar**:			
despertarse	to awaken	**sentarse**	to sit down
empezar	to begin	**nevar**	to snow
pensar	to think		

Group 1 -er verbs			
perder to lose			
pierdo	I lose	**perdemos**	we lose
pierdes	you lose	**perdéis**	you lose
pierde	he/she loses; you lose	**pierden**	they lose; you lose
Verbs like **perder**:			
encender	to light		
entender	to understand		
querer	to want, to like, to love		

Group 1 -ir verbs			
preferir to prefer			
prefiero	I prefer	**preferimos**	we prefer
prefieres	you prefer	**preferís**	you prefer
prefiere	he/she prefers; you prefer	**prefieren**	they prefer; you prefer
Verbs like **preferir**:			
divertirse	to amuse oneself		
sentirse	to feel		

encender

Say or write the following in Spanish:

1 I close the door.
2 I wake up at six.
3 They begin to study at seven.
4 We think that it is silly.
5 I understand what he says.
6 They lose every game.
7 I want to go home.
8 I feel tired.

4. Pensamos que es tonto.   5. Entiendo lo que dice.   6. Pierden todos los partidos.
1. Cierro la puerta.   2. Me despierto a las seis.   3. Empiezan a estudiar a las siete.
7. Quiero irme a casa.   8. Me siento cansado/a.

Group 2

Verbs that change **-o-** or **-u-** to **-ue-**. These can be **-ar**, **-er** or **-ir** verbs.

encontrar

llover

Group 2 -ar verbs

encontrar	to meet, to find		
encuentro	I meet	encontramos	we meet
encuentras	you meet	encontráis	you meet
encuentra	he/she meets; you meet	encuentran	they meet; you meet

Verbs like **encontrar**:

acordarse	to remember	jugar	to play
contar	to tell	volar	to fly
costar	to cost		

Group 2 -er verbs

volver	to return		
vuelvo	I return	volvemos	we return
vuelves	you return	volvéis	you return
vuelve	he/she returns; you return	vuelven	they return; you return

Verbs like **volver**:

doler	to hurt
poder	to be able
llover	to rain

Group 2 -ir verbs

dormir	to sleep		
duermo	I sleep	dormimos	we sleep
duermes	you sleep	dormís	you sleep
duerme	he/she sleeps; you sleep	duermen	they sleep; you sleep

Verbs like **dormir**:

morir	to die

Say or write the following in Spanish:

1 I remember my holidays in Spain.
2 They play tennis on Saturdays.
3 I fly to Spain tomorrow.
4 My arm hurts.
5 It rains in the winter.
6 We return tomorrow.
7 I sleep very well.

6. Volvemos mañana.   7. Duermo muy bien.
3. Vuelo a España mañana.   4. Me duele el brazo.   5. Llueve en invierno.
1. Me acuerdo de mis vacaciones en España.   2. Juegan al tenis los sábados.

49

Group 3

Verbs that change **-e-** to **-i-**.

reír

Group 3			
pedir	to ask (for)		
pido	I ask	**pedimos**	we ask
pides	you ask	**pedís**	you ask
pide	he/she asks; you ask	**piden**	they ask; you ask

Verbs like **pedir**:			
despedirse de	to say goodbye to	**seguir**	to follow
reír	to laugh	**vestirse**	to get dressed
repetir	to repeat		

PROGRESS CHECK

Say or write the following in Spanish:
1. He asks for the bill.
2. I follow my friends.
3. I get dressed and then go out.

1. Pide la cuenta.
2. Sigo a mis amigos.
3. Me visto y salgo.

Irregular verbs (first person only)

Many verbs that are irregular in the present tense are only irregular in the first person singular. After that they are regular.

conducir

hacer	to do, to make
hago	I do
haces	you do
hace	he/she does; you do
hacemos	we do
hacéis	you do
hacen	they do; you do

Other verbs that are irregular in the first person only are:	
caerse (to fall)	**caigo**, **caes**, etc.
conducir (to drive)	**conduzco**, **conduces**, etc.
conocer (to know)	**conozco**, **conoces**, etc.
dar (to give)	**doy**, **das**, etc.
ofrecer (to offer)	**ofrezco**, **ofreces**, etc.
poner (to put)	**pongo**, **pones**, etc.
saber (to know)	**sé**, **sabes**, etc.
salir (to go out)	**salgo**, **sales**, etc.
traer (to bring)	**traigo**, **traes**, etc.
ver (to see)	**veo**, **ves**, etc.

Irregular verbs

The following verbs are irregular throughout the present tense. Unfortunately they are some of the most common verbs in Spanish, so make sure you learn them thoroughly.

decir (to say)	huir (to flee)	ser (to be)
digo	huyo	soy
dices	huyes	eres
dice	huye	es
decimos	huimos	somos
decís	huís	sois
dicen	huyen	son
estar (to be)	ir (to go)	tener (to have)
estoy	voy	tengo
estás	vas	tienes
está	va	tiene
estamos	vamos	tenemos
estáis	vais	tenéis
están	van	tienen
haber (to have (aux.))	oír (to hear)	venir (to come)
he	oigo	vengo
has	oyes	vienes
ha	oye	viene
hemos	oímos	venimos
habéis	oís	venís
han	oyen	vienen

oír

PROGRESS CHECK

Say or write the following in Spanish:
1. I do, I fall, I drive, I know, I give, I offer, I put, I go out, I bring, I see.
2. I say that I am in the dining room.
3. We go if we hear the noise.
4. I am a member and I have a card.

1. Hago, me caigo, conduzco, sé/conozco, doy, ofrezco, pongo, salgo, traigo, veo.
2. Digo que estoy en el comedor. 3. Nos vamos si oímos el ruido. 4. Soy miembro y tengo una tarjeta.

Sample controlled assessment

Speaking

① **Track 9** You are going to have a conversation with your teacher about smoking. Your teacher could ask about…

- whether you smoke
- why you do or do not smoke
- the government's stance
- why young people smoke
- how you feel about passive smoking
- whether you have any advice for youngsters.

Teacher: ¿Fumas?

Student: En absoluto.[16] Es malísimo para la salud. Antes fumaba[13] mucho. Era adicto/a pero después de ver[8] un documental sobre los peligros del tabaco, dejé de fumar. He abandonado el tabaco por completo[16] y nunca[24] fumo. No fumo desde hace[26] dos años.

Teacher: ¿Por qué?

Student: El tabaco contiene ingredientes que[30] son peligrosos para el corazón, la piel y sobre todo para los pulmones así que no tengo ganas[1] de fumar. Los últimos sondeos dan miedo. Ahora hay más chicas que chicos que fuman. Tres chicas de cada diez fuman. A pesar del[19] consejo de sus padres, mi hermana fuma y huele mal. Su ropa huele mal y tiene los dientes y los dedos amarillos. ¡Es tan[18] asqueroso! Pero dice que está a punto de[21] dejar de fumar.

Teacher: Y ¿el gobierno?

Student: Han prohibido los anuncios de tabaco, incluso los anuncios en la tele. Los fabricantes de cigarrillos intentan atraer a los jóvenes. Las multinacionales hasta[16] nos animan a fumar. En Africa distribuyen los cigarrillos gratis. ¡Qué escándalo! ¡Qué pesadilla![9] Desafortunadamente,[16] los fabricantes de cigarrillos financian la Fórmula uno y los jóvenes pueden ver los anuncios en la tele. Debemos decir al gobierno que haga[25] más. Deberían[14] encarecer el tabaco.[22]

Teacher: ¿Por qué fuman tantos jóvenes?

Student: Fuman para parecer[31] más adultos. Hay gente que fuma para ser como sus amigos. Lo[32] hacen para parecer más sofisticados. Es sociable. Dicen que el tabaco les calma los nervios. Lo encuentran relajante y combate el estrés. Si hay un problema, sin perder un momento[5] sacan los cigarrillos.

Teacher: Y ¿lo de fumar de forma pasiva?

Student: Al ver[7] a la gente que fuma, me enfado. Fumar de forma pasiva me preocupa. Soy víctima de esto y ahora soy asmático/a. Nadie[24] tiene derecho de hacer sufrir a los demás.

Teacher: ¿Tienes un consejo para los niños?

Student: Sí. Antes de empezar[6] a fumar, piénsalo bien. Es la peor[23] cosa que puedes hacer. Si decides fumar, será[12] una decisión lamentable.

Turn to page 155 for a translation of this passage.

Examiner's comments

This student has implemented many of the '32 points for improving your grade' from pages 8–9 and is on course for a high grade:

1   A 'tener' structure

5   'Sin' + the infinitive

6   'Antes de…'

7   'Al' + the infinitive

8   'Después de' + the infinitive

9   Two exclamations here

12   A future tense

13   Good use of the imperfect

14   An example of the conditional

16   Impressive vocabulary and structures, e.g. 'en absoluto' is much better than 'no'

18   'Tan' is better than 'muy'

19   'A pesar de'

21   'Estar a punto de'

22   A comparative has been used

23   An example of the superlative

24   Good negatives used

25   A subjunctive has been included

26   A 'desde hace' structure

30   'Que' is a good connective

31   'Para' + the infinitive

32   A pronoun has been used

Sample controlled assessment

Writing

1. Write about your future plans regarding marriage or partnership. You could write about...

   - how you see your future
   - whether you will choose marriage or partnership
   - any other plans you have for the future
   - the importance or otherwise of marriage
   - the attitude of people in your family to marriage.

Voy a describir[12] mi futuro. Voy a ser verdaderamente[18] feliz. Eso será[12] dentro de un año, de dos años o cuando tenga treinta años[25] pero es la felicidad que[30] busco. La[32] encontraré porque[2] viviré mi vida a mi manera.[16] Tengo ganas[1] de casarme.

No voy a casarme antes de la edad de treinta años y tendré por lo menos[16] tres niños. Ser padre/madre forma parte de mis planes aunque[16] tengo miedo[1] de la idea de tener niños. Quiero niños, montones de niños,[16] pero antes de casarme[6] tengo ganas[1] de viajar por todo el mundo. Después de viajar,[8] lo importante es el amor.[16] Viviré en una casa de lujo. Cuando termine[25] mis estudios, espero conocer a una buena pareja. Al conocerle/la,[7] sabré en seguida[16] si es la persona que[30] necesito. Cuando termine[25] la universidad, voy a casarme con una persona especial, quizás[16] una persona famosa. Seré amo/a de casa. Mi pareja seguirá[16] trabajando mientras yo me quedaré en casa a cuidar de los niños.

Para mí, el matrimonio es importante para buenas relaciones. Es un vínculo que une la pareja.[16] Voy a casarme porque es importante que los niños tengan[25] estabilidad. Es la cosa más importante del mundo.[23] Acabo de discutir[20] este tema con mi hermana mayor.[16] Dice ella que no comprende por qué la gente se casa. ¡Qué horror![9]

Dice que es más fácil[22] cohabitar sin casarse.[5] Ella está a punto de[21] ir a vivir con su novio. Yo no cohabitaré nunca[24] a pesar de que[19] mis padres habían vivido juntos[17] antes de casarse.[6] Habían cohabitado durante cinco años. Mi hermano menor no está ni a favor ni[24] en contra del matrimonio pero lamentablemente[16] dice que no quiere niños.

Turn to page 155 for a translation of this passage.

Turn to page 155 for a translation of this passage.

Examiner's comments

This model example uses many of the 32 points from pages 8–9 and would be worth an A*:

1   'Tener' structures
2   'Porque'
5   'Sin' + the infinitive
6   Examples of 'antes de...'
7   'Al' + the infinitive
8   'Después de' + the infinitive
9   An exclamation
12 Examples of future tenses
16 Impressive vocabulary and structures, e.g. 'por lo menos', 'montones de niños', 'quizás', 'mi pareja seguirá', 'mi hermana mayor', 'lamentablemente'
17 An example of the pluperfect
18 'Verdaderamente' has been used
19 'A pesar de'
20 An 'acabar de' structure
21 'Estar a punto de'
22 An example of the comparative
23 A superlative has been included
24 Good examples of negatives
25 Subjunctives have been used. Brilliant!
30 'Que' is a good connecting word
32 A pronoun has been included

Exam practice questions

Listening

1   **Track 10**   Six boys are talking about their families. Match each statement to the correct image and name. Write the name of the correct boy in the spaces provided.

(a) ....   **(b)** ....

(c) ....   **(d)** ....

(e) ....   **(f)** ....   **(6)**

Luis   Enrique   Jaime   Carlos   Rafael   José

2   **Track 11**   Four Spaniards describe themselves. Fill in the boxes.

Name	Favourite subject	Favourite sport	Transport to school
Juan			
Elena			
Sofía			
Enrique			

(12)

3   **Track 12**   You arrive at the home of your Spanish friend. Tick the correct boxes.

(a)   The food is served...

    A   while seeing the room   ☐

    B   after seeing the room   ☐

    C   straight away   ☐

(b)   The room is...

    A   far from here   ☐

    B   quiet   ☐

    C   noisy   ☐

(c)   You can put your things...

    A   in the wardrobe   ☐

    B   on the bed   ☐

    C   under the bed   ☐

Exam practice questions

(d) For dinner there is…

   A meat ☐

   B salad ☐

   C fish ☐

(e) Later you are going to…

   A dance ☐

   B sleep ☐

   C watch TV ☐

(f) Who is coming later?

   A Her sister ☐

   B Her brother ☐

   C Her English friend ☐ **(6)**

Reading

1 Read the e-mail message and answer the questions that follow.

> Querida María
>
> Gracias por el e-mail que me mandaste. Estoy muy decepcionada. ¿Por qué no vienes aquí para aprender inglés? Yo creo que tus planes son una pérdida de dinero. Hay cursos similares en Inglaterra y probablemente son mejores. ¿Por qué no vienes a quedarte conmigo y con mi familia? Es la mejor manera de aprender inglés. Si vienes, iremos a conciertos y visitaremos los sitios interesantes de Londres. Hay otra razón: Peter, el chico a quien conociste el año pasado, quiere verte.
>
> Un abrazo Margaret

(a) Why does Margaret thank María? ....

(b) Why is Margaret disappointed? ....

(c) What does Margaret think of her plans? ....

(d) What is Margaret's opinion of similar courses in England? ....

(e) What is the best way of learning English? ....

(f) Where would they go? ....

(g) Give another reason why María should come. .... **(7)**

Exam practice questions

2 Read the magazine article below about young people and how easy it is to get permission to go out, then answer the questions that follow.

Algunos jóvenes dan sus opiniones sobre sus relaciones con sus padres. He aquí algunos extractos.

¡Quiero salir!

No puedo hacer nada: marcharme el fin de semana, salir una tarde o pasarme por casa de una amiga. Debo hablar por lo menos tres días antes con mis padres y a menudo me dicen que no en el último momento. **Ana, 16 años**

Mis padres no comprenden el hecho de que quiero salir. Para mí, los amigos son mi razón de ser. Mis padres dicen que me debo ganar cada salida, es como una recompensa. Es cansador discutir constantemente. **Pedro, 15 años**

No hay problemas con mis padres respecto a las salidas. Salgo cuando quiero el fin de semana y durante la semana hago los deberes. Simplemente me piden que los avise con antelación cuando pienso volver después de medianoche y también que no vuelva en estado de embriaguez y les garantice que al día siguiente (el domingo) no voy a dormir todo el día. **Édgar, 17 años**

Tengo un acuerdo con mis padres. Puedo elegir 2 fines de semana al mes. Concierto, sala de fiestas o fiesta en casa de los amigos… Es necesario que precise la hora de mi vuelta. Pago mis salidas con mi asignación semanal. Aprendo a hacer elecciones. **María, 16 años**

(a) **(i)** What must Ana do if she wants to go out? ....

      (ii) What might happen at the last moment? .... **(2)**

(b) What is Pedro's reason for living? .... **(1)**

(c) What must Pedro do if he wants to go out? .... **(1)**

(d) What does Pedro find tiring? .... **(1)**

(e) When does Édgar go out? .... **(1)**

(f) Before Édgar goes out, what must he do?

      .... **(1)**

(g) When Édgar gets home, what is expected of him? .... **(1)**

(h) What must Édgar not do on Sundays? .... **(1)**

(i) What bargain has María struck with her parents?

      .... **(1)**

(j) Name the three places María likes to go.

      (i) .... **(ii)** .... **(iii)** .... **(3)**

(k) What must María do before she goes out?

      .... **(1)**

(l) Who pays for María's nights out? .... **(1)**

(m) What has María learned to do? .... **(1)**

Exam practice questions

3   Read this e-mail and answer the questions that follow.

> Pablo
>
> ¿Cómo estás? Volví a Inglaterra sin novedad pero aquí hace muy mal tiempo. Estoy escribiendo para darte las gracias por todo lo que hiciste por mí. El primer desastre ocurrió cuando perdí mi dinero en la playa. Afortunadamente me prestaste dinero. Luego estuve enfermo y no podía hacer nada. Llamaste al médico. Luego hubo un retraso con el vuelo de regreso y me dejaste quedarme una noche más. Aparte de eso, mis vacaciones en España fueron magníficas. Te doy las gracias sinceramente por todo. Espero que te guste el regalo que mando como agradecimiento. El año que viene volveré a España.
>
> Un abrazo Andrew

(a)   What three problems did Andrew have?

     (i)   ....

     (ii)   ....

     (iii)   .... **(3)**

(b)   What three things did Pablo do to solve the problems?

     (i)   ....

     (ii)   ....

     (iii)   .... **(3)**

(c) What is Andrew sending? .... **(1)**

(d) What will happen next year? .... **(1)**

4   Read this e-mail and answer the questions that follow.

> Marta
>
> Mi novio y yo estábamos pasando las vacaciones a orillas del mar y un día decidimos comer un helado porque hacía buen tiempo. Nos sentamos en un muro al lado del puerto. Detrás de nosotros un pescador pescaba con una caña. Al terminar los helados decidimos volver al hotel y nos marchamos en bicicleta. Desafortunadamente nos habíamos dejado una bolsa en el muro con mi móvil dentro. No nos dimos cuenta de lo que habíamos hecho hasta llegar a nuestro hotel. Afortunadamente el pescador había visto lo que había pasado y vino a nuestro hotel con la bolsa. Creo que los españoles son muy simpáticos y le daré un regalo al pescador.
>
> Toni

(a)   Why did Toni sit on the wall? ....

(b)   Who was Toni with? ....

(c)   Where was the wall? ....

(d)   Who was behind them? ....

(e)   What was in Toni's bag? ....

(f)   How did Toni get her bag back? .... **(6)**

Exam practice questions

5 Read this article about a famous person and then answer the questions.

Elena Lang – ¡gran éxito!

Cantante excepcional, a Elena le gusta pasar tiempo con sus amigas cuando salen a bailar. Aunque ahora ha ganado un montón de dinero a Elena le encanta vestir con simplicidad, es decir no gasta dinero en lo que está de moda. Siempre había llevado el pelo corto pero estos días se ha decidido por el pelo largo que le da un aire mucho más sofisticado.

Sus padres emigraron a España de Suecia y nació Elena dos años más tarde. Nació en un barrio pobre de Madrid hace veintidós años pero con su talento excepcional y su voz maravillosa a la edad de 18 años pudo iniciar una serie de conciertos – con gran éxito. Por desgracia tuvo que suspender algunos de ellos porque se encontraba embarazada. Se casó con José Luis Herráiz, pintor y abogado el año pasado y ahora la pareja tiene a Ana y Rosita, gemelas. En otoño del 2008, José Luis expuso por primera vez su colección de pintura y las 10 pinturas se vendieron en dos horas. Al salir de la exposición, una multitud de periodistas le preguntó si estaba enamorado de Elena. "La adoro. Eso es todo lo que tengo que decir" dijo el pintor.

Elena se siente muy orgullosa de sus raíces suecas y visita regularmente a sus parientes de Estocolmo.

Aunque trabaja como una loca – esta semana siete conciertos en siete días – Elena es una persona muy compasiva. Un ejemplo de esta compasión es la visita que hizo al Hospital Madre de Dios, dándoles regalos a los niños enfermos. Un niño a quien visitó fue su primo Daniel y ahora Daniel siempre tiene la foto de Elena en la cabecera de su cama. Daniel tiene las dos piernas rotas: se cayó de su bicicleta. Las heridas son tan graves que los médicos le han dicho que no volverá a caminar nunca más.

(a) What is Elena's profession? .... **(1)**

(b) What does Elena **not** spend her money on? .... **(1)**

(c) Why does Elena look more sophisticated now? .... **(1)**

(d) Where did Elena's parents emigrate from? .... **(1)**

(e) How old is Elena? .... **(1)**

(f) What did Elena do when she was 18? .... **(1)**

(g) Why did Elena have to cancel some concerts? .... **(1)**

(h) What happened to Elena last year? .... **(1)**

(i) What are José Luis's two professions?

    (i) ....   **(ii)** .... **(2)**

(j) What is special about Ana and Rosita? .... **(1)**

(k) What does José Luis say about his relationship with Elena?

    .... **(1)**

(l) Who does Elena visit in Stockholm? .... **(1)**

(m) Why did Elena visit the hospital?

    .... **(1)**

(n) What relation is Daniel to Elena? .... **(1)**

(o) **(i)** How did Daniel hurt himself? ....

    (ii) What have the doctors said? .... **(2)**

3 Leisure, free time and the media

The following topics are covered in this chapter:

- **Free time activities**
- **Shopping, money, fashion and trends**
- **Advantages and disadvantages of new technology**
- **Grammar**

3.1 Free time activities

LEARNING SUMMARY

After studying this section, you should be able to:

- talk about your interests in sport and your hobbies
- give reasons why you like or dislike various sports
- talk about your favourite films and TV programmes
- talk about music and whether you play musical instruments

Sport and leisure

AQA	✓
OCR	✓
EDEXCEL	✓
WJEC	✓
CCEA	✓

Sport and leisure is a favourite topic of examiners. It is likely that you will be asked about your sporting interests in the controlled assessments. You should make sure that you can talk about your favourite sports, and be able to say which sports you like and which you dislike. You must be able to say how you spend your free time, how you spent your free time (for example, last weekend) and how you will spend your free time (for example, next weekend). You will also find the following vocabulary invaluable for the listening and reading exams.

el balonvolea

Sports (Los deportes)

el alpinismo – climbing
el atletismo – athletics
el baloncesto – basketball
el balonmano – handball
el balonvolea – volleyball
el billar – billiards
el ciclismo – cycling
la corrida de toros – bullfight
los deportes de invierno – winter sports
la equitación – horse-riding
el esquí acuático – water-skiing
el fútbol – football

el hockey – hockey
el monopatinaje – skateboarding
la natación – swimming
el patinaje – skating
la pesca – fishing
el ping-pong – table tennis
el rugby – rugby
el tenis – tennis
los toros – bullfighting (literally: 'the bulls')
la vela – sailing
el windsurf – windsurfing

Sports words

el esquí

el balón – ball	**el estadio** – stadium
la bicicleta – bicycle	**el gol** – goal
el campeonato – championship	**el juego** – game
la caña de pescar – fishing rod	**los Juegos Olímpicos** – Olympic Games
la carrera – race	**el partido** – match
el polideportivo – sports centre	**el premio** – prize
el concurso – competition	**el resultado** – result
la Copa del Mundo – World Cup	**el terreno** – pitch
el deporte – sport	**el torneo** – tournament
el esquí – ski, skiing	**la vela** – sail

Sports people (Los/las deportistas)

el/la atleta – athlete	**el/la jugador(a)** – player
el/la campeón/campeona – champion	**el/la matador(a)** – bullfighter (who makes the kill)
el/la ciclista – cyclist	
el/la equipo – team	**el/la tenista** – tennis player
el/la espectador(a) – spectator	**el/la torero/a** – bullfighter
el/la futbolista – footballer	

Free time (El tiempo libre)

las cartas

el bañador – swimsuit	**el juguete** – toy
la canción – song	**la lotería** – lottery
las cartas – playing cards	**la máquina fotográfica** – camera
el CD – CD	**la moda** – fashion
la colección – collection	**el ocio** – free time
la discoteca – disco, club	**el pasatiempo** – hobby
el interés – interest	**los ratos libres** – free time

Leisure activities (Los ocios)

el ajedrez – chess	**la cocina** – cooking
el baile – dance	**el footing** – jogging
los bolos – bowling	**el monopatín** – skateboard
la caza – hunting	**el paseo** – walk
la cerámica – pottery	**el videojuego** – video game

Reading (La lectura)

la ciencia-ficción – science fiction

el diario – newspaper

el libro – book

la novela – novel

el periódico – newspaper

la prensa – press

la revista – magazine

el tebeo – comic

Leisure verbs

patinar

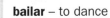

bailar – to dance

cantar – to sing

cazar – to hunt

coleccionar – to collect

dar un paseo – to go for a walk

dar una vuelta – to go for a walk

divertirse – to enjoy oneself

leer – to read

pasarlo bien – to have a good time

pasarlo bomba – to have a great time

pasearse – to go for a walk

patinar – to skate

pescar – to fish

pintar – to paint

tocar – to touch, to play

PROGRESS CHECK

Say or write the following in Spanish:

1. Fishing
2. Game
3. Athlete
4. Toy
5. Jogging
6. Reading
7. I like going for walks.
8. I do not like painting.
9. I prefer fishing.

1. La pesca   2. El juego   3. El/la atleta   4. El juguete   5. El footing   6. La lectura   7. Me gusta dar paseos.   8. No me gusta pintar.   9. Prefiero la pesca.

Conversation

AQA	✓
OCR	✓
EDEXCEL	✓
WJEC	✓
CCEA	✓

The following are commonly-asked questions in the speaking assessment. Practise these sentences with a friend.

1 You should add a few more hobbies, e.g. 'y ver la tele'.

¿Cuál es tu pasatiempo favorito?

Me gusta jugar al tenis.[1]

¿Dónde juegas al tenis?

Juego en el parque.

¿Con quién juegas?

Juego con un amigo.

¿Te gusta la jardinería?

Odio la jardinería.

¿Qué deportes practicas?

Juego al hockey/al fútbol.

Conversation

AQA	✓
OCR	✓
EDEXCEL	✓
WJEC	✓
CCEA	✓

¿Quieres describir tus pasatiempos?

Tengo muchos pasatiempos. Me gusta jugar al fútbol/hockey/tenis/baloncesto. También me gusta leer, ver la televisión, ir al cine y salir con mis amigos.

1 Your chance to show you know the present tense.

2 Your chance to show you know the preterite tense (see pages 93–94).

3 Your chance to show you know the future tense (see pages 123–124).

🔊 **¿Cuál es tu deporte favorito?**

💬 **Mi deporte favorito es la natación. Normalmente voy a la piscina los sábados con mis amigos.**

🔊 **¿Qué lees?**

💬 **Me gusta leer novelas pero también leo revistas y periódicos.**

🔊 **¿Qué haces normalmente por la tarde después de tus deberes?[1]**

💬 **Leo, veo la televisión, escucho música, doy un paseo con el perro y visito a mis amigos.**

🔊 **¿Qué hiciste anoche después de tus deberes?[2]**

💬 **Leí, vi la televisión, escuché música, di un paseo con el perro y visité a un amigo.**

🔊 **¿Qué harás esta tarde después de tus deberes?[3]**

💬 **Leeré, veré la televisión, escucharé música, daré un paseo con el perro y visitaré a un amigo.**

Cinema and TV

AQA	✓
OCR	✓
EDEXCEL	✓
WJEC	✓
CCEA	✓

Films and TV is a likely topic for your controlled assessments. You will probably be asked about your favourite type of film or TV programme. In the reading exam, you might be given a TV schedule or a film schedule and asked questions about which programmes are shown at which times.

Cinema and theatre (El cine y el teatro)

la comedia – comedy

los dibujos animados – cartoon

la estrella del cine – cinema star

el éxito – success

la localidad – seat, ticket

la obra de teatro – play

la película – film

la película de amor – romantic film

la película de aventuras – adventure film

la película de ciencia-ficción – science-fiction film

la película de guerra – war film

la película de miedo – horror film

la película del oeste – western

la película policíaca – detective film

la sesión – performance

TV (La tele)

la radio

el/la actor/actriz – actor/actress

la charla – chat

el documental – documentary

el DVD – DVD

el episodio – episode

las noticias – news

la pantalla – screen

el programa – programme

la publicidad – advertising

la radio – radio

el telediario – TV news

la telenovela – soap

la TVE – Spanish TV channel

el vídeo – video

PROGRESS CHECK

Say or write the following in Spanish:

1 Film

2 Soap

3 I like watching films on TV.

4 I prefer horror films.

1. La película
2. La telenovela
3. Me gusta ver las películas en la tele.
4. Prefiero las películas de miedo.

Music and musical instruments

AQA	✓
OCR	✓
EDEXCEL	✓
WJEC	✓
CCEA	✓

If your teacher knows that you like music or that you play an instrument, you may well be asked about music in your controlled speaking assessment. You need to be able to express your likes, dislikes and preferences. You might like to use a famous musician as the subject for your presentation, if you are doing one, or for your controlled writing assessment. The following vocabulary will also help you in the listening and reading exams.

Music (La música)

la canción – song
el concierto – concert
el disco compacto – CD
el estéreo – stereo
el grupo – group
el instrumento – instrument

la música clásica – classical music
la música alta – loud music
la música pop – pop music
el/la músico/a – musician
la orquesta – orchestra
sé tocar... – I can play...

la flauta

Musical instruments (Los instrumentos musicales)

las castañuelas – castinets
la flauta – flute
la flauta dulce – recorder
la guitarra – guitar

el piano – piano
la trompeta – trumpet
el violín – violin

PROGRESS CHECK

Say or write the following in Spanish:

1 CD
2 Guitar
3 To sing
4 I went to a classical music concert last night.
5 I love pop music.
6 I play the flute.

1. El disco compacto 2. La guitarra 3. Cantar 4. Anoche fui a un concierto de música clásica. 5. Me encanta la música pop. 6. Toco la flauta./Sé tocar la flauta.

Conversation

AQA	✓
OCR	✓
EDEXCEL	✓
WJEC	✓
CCEA	✓

Your chance to give an opinion and to justify it.

🎵 **¿Sabes tocar un instrumento musical?**
🎵 Sé tocar la guitarra.
🎵 **¿Qué tipo de música te gusta?**
🎵 Me gusta la música pop.
🎵 **¿Qué tipo de película te gusta?**
🎵 Me gustan las películas de aventura. No me gustan las películas de horror ni las películas de guerra porque son demasiado violentas.

3.2 Shopping, money, fashion and trends

LEARNING SUMMARY

After studying this section, you should be able to:

- talk about shops and shopping
- talk about the post office, bank and money
- describe clothes, fashion and trends

Shops and shopping

AQA ✓
OCR ✓
EDEXCEL ✓
WJEC ✓
CCEA ✓

The following vocabulary will help you in the listening and reading exams, and in the controlled assessment.

Shops (Las tiendas)

la agencia de viajes – travel agent
la biblioteca – library
la carnicería – butcher's
correos (m, sing) – post office
el estanco – tobacconist's
la farmacia – chemist's
la frutería – fruit shop
la hamburguesería – hamburger outlet
la joyería – jeweller's
la librería – bookshop
el mercado – market
la panadería – baker's

la papelería – stationer's
la pastelería – cake shop
la peluquería – hairdresser's
la perfumería – perfume shop
la pescadería – fishmonger's
la relojería – watch maker's
el supermercado – supermarket
la tienda de comestibles – grocer's
la tienda de recuerdos – souvenir shop
la tienda de ultramarinos – grocer's
la verdulería – greengrocer's
la zapatería – shoe shop

la peluquería

el carro

el escaparate

Shopping (Las compras)

la alimentación – food
los almacenes – stores
la bolsa – bag
el bolso – handbag
la caja – cash desk
el carro – supermarket trolley
el/la cesto/a – basket
el/la cliente – customer
la cola – queue
los comestibles – food
el/la dependiente/a – shop assistant

el descuento – discount
el dinero – money
el escaparate – shop window
la liquidación – sale
el precio – price
las rebajas – reductions
el recuerdo – souvenir
la talla – size
la tienda – shop
el/la vendedor(a) – salesperson

hacer cola

Shopping verbs

comprar – to buy
costar – to cost
envolver – to wrap up
gastar – to spend (money)

hacer cola – to queue
introducir – to insert
ir de compras – to go shopping

mirar – to look at
pagar – to pay
vender – to sell

At the bank (En el banco)

el billete de banco – banknote
el cajero automático – cashpoint
el cambio – change
el cheque de viaje – traveller's cheque

la comisión – commission
el dinero – money
la libra esterlina – pound (sterling)
la moneda – coin, currency
la tarjeta de crédito – credit card

Conversation

AQA	✓
OCR	✓
EDEXCEL	✓
WJEC	✓
CCEA	✓

¿Vas de compras con tus amigos?

Sí, me encanta ir de compras.

¿Qué compras?

Compro ropa, comida y bebida.

¿Qué comida y bebida te gusta comprar?

Me gusta comprar dulces y gaseosa.

¿Ahorras dinero?

Cada semana ingreso 10 euros en el banco. Ahorro dinero para poder comprar un ordenador, un reproductor de MP3, y para ir de vacaciones.

Y ¿en qué gastas el resto de tu dinero?

Cuando salgo me lo pago todo yo, compro CDs, maquillaje, ropa y clases de conducir. De vez en cuando doy dinero a una organización benéfica que ayuda a los animales.

KEY POINT

Ahorrar means 'to save' (money or time) but to save someone (e.g. from drowning) is **salvar**. To save something on the computer is **guardar**.

PROGRESS CHECK

Say or write the following in Spanish:

1. Supermarket
2. Baker's
3. Fishmonger's
4. Sale
5. Price
6. Size
7. Reductions
8. Where is the butcher's?
9. Credit card
10. Money
11. I would like to change some traveller's cheques.

1. El supermercado 2. La panadería 3. La pescadería 4. La liquidación 5. El precio 6. La talla 7. Las rebajas 8. ¿Dónde está la carnicería? 9. La tarjeta de crédito 10. El dinero 11. Quiero cambiar cheques de viaje.

Fashion and trends

AQA	✓
OCR	✓
EDEXCEL	✓
WJEC	✓
CCEA	✓

Clothes (La ropa)

el **abrigo** – overcoat
la **blusa** – blouse
el **bolso** – bag
las **botas** – boots
la **bufanda** – scarf
los **calcetines** – socks
la **camisa** – shirt
la **camiseta** – t-shirt
la **chaqueta** – jacket
el **cinturón** – belt
la **corbata** – tie
la **falda** – skirt
los **guantes** – gloves
el **impermeable** – raincoat

la **marca** – make
las **medias** – tights
los **pantalones** – trousers
los **pantalones cortos** – shorts
el **paraguas** – umbrella
las **deportivas** – trainers
el **probador** – changing room
probarse – to try on
las **sandalias** – sandals
el **sombrero** – hat
la **talla** – size (clothes)
los **vaqueros** – jeans
el **vestido** – dress
los **zapatos** – shoes

de lana

Materials (Los materiales)

de **algodón** – cotton
de **cuero** – leather
de **lana** – wool
de **nylon** – nylon

de **seda** – silk
de **terciopelo** – velvet
de **tergal/polyester** – polyester

Colours (Los colores)

amarillo/a – yellow
azul – blue
blanco/a – white
claro/a – light
crema – cream
gris – grey
marrón – brown

morado/a – purple
naranja – orange
negro/a – black
oscuro/a – dark
rojo/a – red
rosa – pink
verde – green

KEY POINT

Naranja, **rosa** and **crema** never change their endings.

un jersey holgado

Style (El estilo)

la **blusa con puntitos amarillos** – spotty yellow blouse
la **blusa rayada** – striped blouse
la **camisa lisa** – plain shirt
corto – short
el **efecto mojado** – wet look
la **falda ajustada** – tight skirt

la **falda de cuadros escoceses** – tartan skirt
el **jersey holgado** – baggy jumper
largo – long
la **minifalda a cuadros** – checked miniskirt
la **moda 'rapper'** – rapper look
siniestro/a – goth

- **Un cuadro** really means 'a square' in **la minifalda a cuadros**. **La falda de cuadros escoceses** literally means 'the skirt of Scottish checks'.
- Instead of **la blusa rayada**, you can say **la blusa a rayas**. **La blusa con puntitos amarillos** refers to the spots themselves being yellow.

Out shopping

Un pantalón de cuero no te queda bien.

Leather trousers do not suit you.

Busco una camisa de seda.

I am looking for a silk shirt.

¿Qué talla tiene?

What size are you?

Calzo el número 10.

I take a size 10 (shoes).

Número means 'size' for shoes. Everything else is **talla**.

Busco zapatillas de deporte.

I am looking for trainers.

¿Puedo probármelo?

Can I try it on?

'To try on' is **probarse**. 'To try out' (e.g. a new food) is **probar**.

¿Dónde están los probadores?

Where are the changing rooms?

¿Tiene la misma camisa en rojo?

Have you got the same shirt in red?

Lo siento pero no nos quedan.

I am sorry, we haven't got any more.

Other useful sentences

Lleva ropa oscura y botas negras.

He wears dark clothes and black boots.

Lleva una camiseta holgada y un pantalón demasiado largo con zapatillas azules.

He wears a baggy t-shirt and trousers that are too long with blue trainers.

Para ir a su trabajo, va a comprar…

To go to work, she is going to buy…

Para asistir a la boda de su hermana, va a llevar…

To attend her sister's wedding, she is going to wear…

Asistir means 'to assist', but it also means 'to attend'.

Me pongo mi chaqueta nueva.
I am putting on my new jacket.
Se pone un pantalón porque no le gusta llevar faldas.
She is putting on trousers because she does not like wearing skirts.

Conversation

AQA	✓
OCR	✓
EDEXCEL	✓
WJEC	✓
CCEA	✓

- ¿Te gusta ir a la moda?
- Me encanta ir a la moda pero cuesta mucho dinero.
- ¿Gastarías más para tener ropa de diseño/de marca?
- Claro. Tengo que ir a la moda.
- ¿Prefieres la marca escrita delante, detrás o en la etiqueta?
- En la espalda.
- ¿Grande, pequeña o minúscula?
- Grande.
- ¿Qué estilo prefieres, el 'rapper', el siniestro o algún otro?
- Los dos me fascinan pero prefiero mi propio estilo.
- ¿Buscas en la etiqueta 'fabricado en Europa' o compras ropa fabricada por obreros africanos que ganan ocho euros al día?
- Compro sólo Nike y Adidas.

> **KEY POINT**
>
> **Diseño** means 'design' or 'designer'.

3.3 Advantages and disadvantages of new technology

LEARNING SUMMARY	**After studying this section, you should be able to:** - talk about computers, mobile phones and other gadgets - explain the advantages of new technology - explain the disadvantages of new technology

New technology

AQA	✓
OCR	✓
EDEXCEL	✓
WJEC	✓
CCEA	✓

The following vocabulary and sentences will help you in the listening and reading exams, and in the controlled assessment.

ICT (La informática)

el ratón

el archivo – file

la banda ancha – broadband

la barra espaciadora – space bar

borrar – to delete

el buscador – search engine

la cámara digital – digital camera

conectarse a Internet – to log on

la contraseña – password

el cursor – cursor

descargar – to download

el disco duro – hard drive

el DVD – DVD

el e-mail – e-mail

el escáner – scanner

la impresora laser – laser printer

imprimir – to print

el/la Internet – Internet

el lector de CD – CD player

el móvil – mobile phone

navegar en la Web – to surf the Web

el ordenador portátil – laptop

pulsar dos veces – to double-click

el ratón – mouse

el SMS, el mensaje de texto – text

el teclado – keyboard

la Web – the Web

The advantages of new technology – what people say

Internet en el instituto es maravilloso porque nos ayuda con los deberes.

The Internet at school is great because it helps us with our homework.

Tenemos nuestra propia página web.

We have our own website.

Es una manera excelente de comunicarse con otra gente.

It is a marvellous way of communicating with other people.

Me gusta navegar en la Web y jugar.

I like surfing the Web and playing.

Internet es útil si quieres ponerte en contacto con jóvenes de todo el mundo.

The Internet is useful if you want to contact young people anywhere in the world.

Nos permite encontrar contactos y practicar otras lenguas.

It allows us to find contacts and to practise different languages.

> **KEY POINT**
>
> **Lengua** and **idioma** both mean 'language'. **Lengua** is feminine but **idioma** is masculine even though it ends in **-a**.

Pronto vamos a crear nuestra propia página web.

We are soon going to create our own website.

Es útil y no hace ruido.

It is useful and doesn't make any noise.

Mis padres están más tranquilos porque pueden llamarme cuando quieran.

My parents are less worried because they can call me whenever they want.

Con mi móvil nuevo puedo navegar en la Web.

With my new mobile I can surf the Web.

Tengo un móvil con una cámara de cinco megapixels.

My mobile phone has a five megapixel camera.

Tengo un MP3 que es muy ligero con pantalla táctil.

I have an MP3 player that is very light and has a touch screen.

Puedo descargar videoclips gratis.

I can download free video clips.

Mando e-mails, descargo videoclips y juego con videojuegos.

I send e-mails, I download video clips and I play video games.

Busco información en Internet.

I look for information on the Internet.

Para mí, es la mejor manera de encontrar a amigos.

For me, it is the best way of finding friends.

Los móviles son útiles para tu propia seguridad.

Mobiles are useful for your own security.

The disadvantages of new technology – what people say

La desventaja es que tenemos un sólo ordenador en cada clase.

The disadvantage is that we only have one computer per class.

> **KEY POINT**
>
> **La ventaja** is 'advantage' and **la desventaja** is 'disadvantage'.

Por desgracia el sistema informático está muchas veces averiado.

Unfortunately the ICT system is often out of order.

Las páginas desaparecen demasiado deprisa.

The sites disappear too quickly.

Mucha gente pasa demasiado tiempo delante de su ordenador.

Many people spend too much time at the computer.

Hacen menos deporte.

They do less sport.

Va a tener problemas de vista.

He is going to have eyesight problems.

La única cosa que le interesa es su ordenador.

The only thing that he is interested in is his computer.

No juega más al fútbol. Empieza a ser travieso.

He does not play football anymore. He is beginning to get naughty.

Quiere comer comida rápida delante del ordenador.

He wants to eat fast-food in front of the computer.

Se ha vuelto solitario y triste. Ha perdido a sus amigos.

He is becoming a loner and sad. He has lost his friends.

Hay que limitar el acceso a Internet.

You have to limit access to the Internet.

Hay que limitar el tiempo a un cierto número de horas.

You have to limit time to a fixed period.

¿Los móviles son peligrosos para la salud? Los científicos no están seguros. ¡Cuidado!

Are mobiles harmful to your health? Scientists are not sure. Be careful!

Cinco millones de SMSs circulan cada día. Los estudiantes los escriben durante sus clases.

Five million texts are sent every day. Pupils write them during their lessons.

Si te comunicas con desconocidos, hay que dar un nombre falso. No debes dar tu número ni tu dirección.

If you communicate with strangers, you must give a false name. You must not give out your number or your address.

Mis padres se enfadan cuando ven la factura.

My parents get angry when they see the bill.

La gente utiliza su móvil en el tren. Habla en voz alta. ¡Me fastidia!

People use mobiles on trains. They talk loudly. It bothers me!

> **KEY POINT**
>
> **Gente** is singular in Spanish.

Me siento observado/a en todo momento. Mi madre me llama por teléfono para saber dónde estoy.

I feel watched at every moment. My mother calls to find out where I am.

He perdido mi móvil tres veces.

I have lost my mobile three times.

Mucha gente usa su móvil cuando conduce. Provoca muchos accidentes.

Many people use their mobiles when they are driving. It causes a lot of accidents.

Las llamadas al extranjero son muy caras.

Calls abroad are very expensive.

No puedo vivir sin mi móvil pero la factura al fin del mes es cara.

I cannot live without my mobile but the bill at the end of the month is expensive.

Dicen que los móviles son peligrosos para el cerebro.

They say that mobiles are bad for your brain.

Mi MP3 no tiene mucha memoria y tengo que cambiar las pilas cada día.

My MP3 player does not have much memory and I have to change the batteries every day.

> **KEY POINT**
>
> **Pila** is 'a small battery'. The battery in a car is **la batería**.

El fraude es un gran problema.

Fraud is a big problem.

> **PROGRESS CHECK**
>
> Say or write the following in Spanish:
> 1. We are soon going to create our own website.
> 2. Mobiles are very useful.
> 3. You have to limit time to a fixed period.
> 4. He has lost his friends.
> 5. Be careful!
>
> 5. ¡Cuidado!
> 4. Ha perdido a sus amigos.
> 3. Hay que limitar el tiempo a un cierto número de horas.
> 2. Los móviles son muy útiles.
> 1. Pronto vamos a crear nuestra propia página web.

3.4 Grammar

After studying this section, you should be able to understand:

* the perfect tense
* adjectives
* adverbs

The perfect tense

AQA	✓
OCR	✓
EDEXCEL	✓
WJEC	✓
CCEA	✓

> **KEY POINT**
>
> The perfect tense in English always has 'has' or 'have' in it, e.g. I have gone, they have run, he has seen.

The perfect tense in Spanish is formed by taking the present tense of **haber** and adding the past participle. So, you need to know about **haber** and you need to know about past participles.

Present tense of haber

he	I have
has	you have
ha	he/she/it has; you have (polite form)
hemos	we have
habéis	you have
han	they have; you have (polite form)

> **KEY POINT**
>
> Remember that **haber** is only used as an auxiliary verb. To say 'have' in the sense of owning something, use **tener**.

Past participles

To find a past participle of a verb in English, just imagine that the words 'I have' are in front of it. For the verb 'to write', you would say 'I have written', so 'written' is the past participle of 'to write'. In the same way, 'gone' is the past participle of 'to go' and so on.

Formation of past participles in Spanish

Take off the ending (**-ar**, **-er** or **-ir**) and add:

-ado for **-ar** verbs
-ido for **-er** and **-ir** verbs

hablar	➡	**hablado**
comer	➡	**comido**
vivir	➡	**vivido**

Here is the perfect tense of three regular verbs.

hablar	
he hablado	I have spoken
has hablado	you have spoken
ha hablado	he/she/it has spoken; you have spoken
hemos hablado	we have spoken
habéis hablado	you have spoken
han hablado	they have spoken; you have spoken

comer	
he comido	I have eaten
has comido	you have eaten
ha comido	he/she/it has eaten; you have eaten
hemos comido	we have eaten
habéis comido	you have eaten
han comido	they have eaten; you have eaten

vivir	
he vivido	I have lived
has vivido	you have lived
ha vivido	he/she/it has lived; you have lived
hemos vivido	we have lived
habéis vivido	you have lived
han vivido	they have lived; you have lived

comer

Irregular past participles

Some past participles do not obey the rules and must be learned separately.

escribir

abrir (to open)	**he abierto** (I have opened)
cubrir (to cover)	**he cubierto** (I have covered)
decir (to say)	**he dicho** (I have said)
descubrir (to discover)	**he descubierto** (I have discovered)
escribir (to write)	**he escrito** (I have written)
hacer (to do/make)	**he hecho** (I have done/made)
morir (to die)	**ha muerto** (he has died)
poner (to put)	**he puesto** (I have put)
romper (to break)	**he roto** (I have broken)
ver (to see)	**he visto** (I have seen)
volver (to return)	**he vuelto** (I have returned)

PROGRESS CHECK

Say or write the following in Spanish:
1. I have written a letter.
2. He has broken the vase.
3. They have seen the film.

1. He escrito una carta.
2. Ha roto el florero.
3. Han visto la película.

Adjectives

● Adjectives ending in **-o** change as follows:

	Masculine	Feminine
Singular	**blanco**	**blanca**
Plural	**blancos**	**blancas**

● Adjectives ending in **-e** or in a consonant do not change in the feminine singular, e.g.:

	Masculine	Feminine
Singular	**verde** **azul**	**verde** **azul**
Plural	**verdes** **azules**	**verdes** **azules**

● Adjectives of nationality do not follow the above rule, e.g.:

	Masculine	Feminine
Singular	**español**	**española**
Plural	**españoles**	**españolas**

● Some adjectives (**bueno**, **malo**, **alguno**, **ninguno**, **primero**, **tercero**) drop the final **-o** before a masculine singular noun, and **algún** and **ningún** require an accent, e.g.:

un buen/mal hombre	a good/bad man
algún/ningún dinero	some/no money
el primer/tercer ejemplo	the first/third example

● **Grande** becomes **gran** before a masculine or feminine singular noun, e.g.:

un gran hombre	a great man
una gran mujer	a great woman

● Some adjectives change their meaning according to their position, e.g.:

su antiguo amigo	his former friend
el edificio antiguo	the ancient building
el pobre chico	the poor boy (i.e. unfortunate)
el chico pobre	the poor boy (i.e. without any money)
la misma cosa	the same thing
el rey mismo	the king himself (usually used only with people)

● **Cada** (each) never changes, e.g.:

cada niño	each boy
cada niña	each girl

This is a good and easy way of picking up marks in your controlled writing assessment.

● The endings **-ísimo**, **-ísima**, **-ísimos**, **-ísimas** can be added to adjectives after the final vowel is removed to give the meaning 'extremely', e.g.:

un chico guapo	a handsome boy
un chico guapísimo	an extremely handsome boy

PROGRESS CHECK

Say or write the following in Spanish:

1. A pretty girl
2. A red car
3. Two red cars
4. A good teacher
5. Each person
6. An extremely pretty girl
7. The same driver
8. The driver himself

1. Una chica guapa   2. Un coche rojo   3. Dos coches rojos   4. Un buen profesor   5. Cada persona   6. Una chica guapísima   7. El mismo conductor   8. El conductor mismo

Adverbs

AQA ✓
OCR ✓
EDEXCEL ✓
WJEC ✓
CCEA ✓

KEY POINT

In English, most adverbs end in **-ly**, e.g. slowly, quickly, carefully, briefly.

To form an adverb in Spanish, take the feminine form of the adjective and add **-mente**, e.g.:

lento (slow) ➡ **lentamente** (slowly)
cuidadoso (careful) ➡ **cuidadosamente** (carefully)
rápido (fast) ➡ **rápidamente** (quickly)

The same rule applies if the adjective ends in **-e** or a consonant, e.g.:

breve (brief) ➡ **brevemente** (briefly)
normal (normal) ➡ **normalmente** (normally)

KEY POINT

Some adverbs are irregular and do not end in **-mente**:
bien (well)
mal (badly)
despacio (slowly)

> Try to use as many of these adverbs as you can in your controlled writing and speaking assessments.

Learn these adverbs:

- **a menudo** (often), e.g.:
  ¿Vas a menudo al cine? Do you often go to the cinema?
- **de repente** (suddenly), e.g.:
  El coche frenó de repente. The car braked suddenly.
- **desgraciadamente/por desgracia** (unfortunately), e.g.:
  Desgraciadamente/Por desgracia murió. Unfortunately he died.
- **en seguida** (immediately), e.g.:
  Se fue en seguida. He left immediately.
- **luego** (then), e.g.:
  Comió un bocadillo, luego salió. He ate a sandwich, then went out.
- **por tanto/por consiguiente** (so (= therefore)), e.g.:
  Llovía y por tanto/por consiguiente no salí. It was raining and so I didn't go out.
- **pronto** (soon), e.g.:
  Pronto se va de vacaciones. He is soon going on holiday.
- **siempre** (always), e.g.:
  Siempre llega tarde. He always arrives late.

Sample controlled assessment

Speaking

1 Track 13 You are going to have a conversation with your teacher about what you like doing. Your teacher could ask about…

- what you like doing
- what sports you like
- another activity you do
- whether you like reading.

Teacher: ¿Qué te gusta hacer?

Student: Lo que me gusta más[16] es el deporte. Me gustan todos los deportes pero mi favorito es el tenis. Juego al tenis desde hace diez años,[26] es decir casi toda mi vida.[16] Mis padres me[32] animaron a jugar porque[2] ellos también juegan. Decidí[4] hacerme socio de un club cuando tenía ocho años[13] y acabo de ganar[20] mi primer torneo.

Teacher: ¿Te gustan otros deportes?

Student: Estoy a punto de[21] hacerme socio de un club de equitación. Mis padres me regalaron un caballo el año pasado. ¡Qué sorpresa![9] Es el caballo más hermoso del mundo.[23] Es tan inteligente.[18] Empecé a montar a caballo cuando tenía diez años pero lo había dejado de hacer[17] porque no tenía ni caballo ni dinero.[24]

Teacher: ¿Qué otra actividad te gusta?

Student: Me gustan las películas y el cine. Los sábados por la tarde, aunque[25] tenga poco dinero, voy al cine y mi hermano menor[16] me acompaña. Antes de ir,[6] busco las mejores películas[23] en Internet. Después de encontrar[8] una buena película, vamos al centro a verla. A mi hermano le gustan las películas de miedo mientras[30] yo prefiero los dramas.

Teacher: ¿Te gusta leer?

Student: Cuando termino mis deberes, siempre tengo ganas[1] de leer. Sin perder un momento,[5] cojo una novela y leo. No veo nunca[24] la tele. Tantos programas[16] son tan estúpidos.[18] ¡Qué pérdida de tiempo![9] Mi hermano ve cualquier programa[16] a pesar de[19] que la mayoría son estúpidos.

Turn to page 155 for a translation of this passage.

Turn to page 155 for a translation of this passage.

Examiner's comments

You have to speak for four to six minutes in the controlled assessment. The example given here would take two or three minutes, but you could include holidays as one of the things you like doing and talk for another two minutes or so on that topic (see Chapter 4, pages 87–106). This student is on course for a good grade having implemented most of the 32 points on pages 8–9:

2 'Porque'

4 'Decidí' + the infinitive

5 'Sin' + the infinitive

6 'Antes de…'

8 'Después de' + the infinitive

9 Exclamations

13 An example of the imperfect

18 Examples of the use of 'tan'

16 Impressive vocabulary and structures, e.g. 'lo que me gusta más', 'mi hermano menor', 'tantos programas'

17 A pluperfect has been included

19 An 'a pesar de' structure

20 'Acabar de'

21 'Estar a punto de'

23 Superlatives have been used

24 Examples of negatives

25 A subjunctive. Very impressive!

26 A 'desde hace' structure

30 'Mientras' is a good connective

32 A pronoun has been used

Sample controlled assessment

If you have been entered with WJEC, you will have to do a presentation as part of your controlled speaking assessment. If you have been entered with Edexcel, you have to do two from…

- a presentation and discussion
- an open interaction
- a picture-based discussion.

For both WJEC and Edexcel, the presentation is for two to three minutes on a topic of your choice. Then you will be asked questions about your presentation for three to five minutes. You can choose the title of your presentation, but you must discuss it with your teacher before you start preparing. An extract from a sample presentation is shown below. You should not use it yourself because your presentation must be your own work and it would have to be longer than this. However, it might give you ideas.

   Mi deporte favorito

Voy a hablar de mi deporte favorito: el tenis. Jugué al tenis por primera vez cuando tenía ocho años y me encantó en seguida. Pedí una raqueta a mis padres y me regalaron una como regalo de cumpleaños. Tengo suerte porque cerca de mi casa hay unas pistas de tenis y solía ir con mi hermana a jugar todos los fines de semana. Ahora soy miembro de un club de tenis y no sólo me da la ocasión de mantenerme en buena condición física sino que también me da la oportunidad de conocer a gente interesante de mi edad.

También me encanta el tenis profesional y veo los partidos en la televisión. En verano paso muchas horas viendo el torneo de Wimbledon y los otros torneos por todo el mundo. Este año iré a Wimbledon si consigo entradas. Un día me gustaría ser tenista profesional. Mi estrella favorita es Carole Dace…

Here is a translation of the passage above.

My favourite sport

I am going to talk about my favourite sport: tennis. I played tennis for the first time when I was eight and I immediately loved it. I asked my parents for a racquet and they gave me one for my birthday. I am lucky because near my house there are courts and I used to go and play with my sister every weekend. Now I am a member of a tennis club and not only do I get the chance to stay fit, but I also get the chance to meet interesting people of my age.

I also love professional tennis and I watch the games on TV. In summer I spend many hours watching Wimbledon and the other competitions around the world. This year I will go to Wimbledon if I can get tickets. One day I would like to be a professional tennis player. My favourite star is Carole Dace…

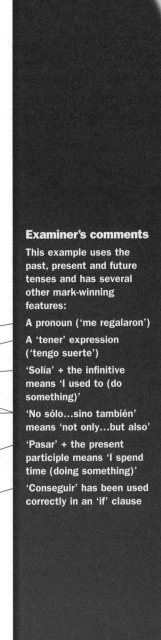

Examiner's comments

This example uses the past, present and future tenses and has several other mark-winning features:

A pronoun ('me regalaron')

A 'tener' expression ('tengo suerte')

'Solía' + the infinitive means 'I used to (do something)'

'No sólo…sino también' means 'not only…but also'

'Pasar' + the present participle means 'I spend time (doing something)'

'Conseguir' has been used correctly in an 'if' clause

Sample controlled assessment

Tips on preparing a presentation

- Use illustrative material. This means that if you want to talk about a book, an article, a photo, a postcard or a small object, you should take that item into the controlled assessment. The candidate on the previous page could take in a photo of the tennis player and say 'He aquí una foto de Carole'. You can then point out things during your presentation, and your teacher will ask you questions on them.

- Spend time preparing your cue card. Look at the '32 points for improving your grade' on pages 8–9. Use as many as you can.

- Your teacher will be looking out for the following things:

    - Use of past, present and future tenses. The exam boards do recognise that it may be difficult for you to use all three in the presentation, but you should try. Bear this in mind when choosing the title of your presentation.
    - Unusual vocabulary and structures.
    - Your ability to give a good presentation, and your ability to answer any unpredictable questions your teacher asks.

- Choose the title of your controlled speaking assessment presentation carefully. Do not choose 'Myself', because it is too broad and may overlap with other topics during the controlled speaking assessment. Some suggestions might be:

    - mi revista favorita
    - mi profesor(a) favorito/a
    - mi hermano/a
    - el intercambio
    - mi deporte favorito
    - mi música favorita
    - mi estrella favorita
    - mi pasatiempo favorito
    - mi deporte favorito

- Be prepared for your teacher to develop the presentation. With the example on the previous page, he/she might ask you these questions:

  ¿Cuántas veces a la semana juegas al tenis?
  ¿Contra quién juegas?
  Describe tu club de tenis.
  ¿Cuánto cuesta?
  Háblame de tu estrella favorita.

Sample controlled assessment

(3) Why not do your presentation on a famous person – a footballer or pop or film star? You could follow this plan:

- *Introducción* (introduction)
- *He escogido a esta persona porque…*
  (I have chosen this person because…)
- *Descripción física* (physical description)
- *Lo que ha hecho* (what he/she has done)
- *Su personalidad* (his/her personality)

Introducción

Voy a hablar de…	I am going to talk about…
Nació en … en mil novecientos setenta y tres.	He/She was born in … in 1973.
Murió en … a la edad de … .	He/She died in … at the age of … .
Vive en … con su esposa /marido/hijos.	He/She lives in … with his/her wife/husband/children.
…es muy especial porque…	…is very special because…
Es famoso/a en todo el mundo.	He/She is famous all over the world.
Es una persona excepcional.	He/She is an exceptional person.

He escogido a esta persona porque…

Me encanta el fútbol/el cine/el deporte/la música rock.	I like football/cinema/sport/rock music.
También juego al fútbol/veo el fútbol en la tele/soy aficionado/a al Wolves.	I also play football/watch football on TV/am a Wolves supporter.
Voy al cine una vez a la semana.	I go to the cinema once a week.
He asistido a muchos de sus conciertos.	I have been to many of his/her concerts.

Descripción física

Es alto/a/de altura media.	He/She is tall/medium size.
Tiene el pelo largo y negro/ corto y castaño.	He/She has long, black/short, brown hair.
Ahora es calvo.	Now he is bald.
Tiene los ojos azules/verdes.	He/She has blue/green eyes.

Examiner's comments

Take a photo into the controlled assessment and point out the characteristics.

Sample controlled assessment

Lo que ha hecho

Es un futbolista famoso.	He is a famous footballer.
Es un(a) cantante estupendo/a.	He/She is a fantastic singer.
Canta música rock y ha grabado muchos CDs.	He/She sings rock music and has made many CDs.
Es estrella del cine.	He/She is a film star.
Me ha ayudado mucho.	He/She has helped me a lot.
Marcó muchísimos goles.	He/She has scored a lot of goals.
Ha hecho muchísimas películas estupendas.	He/She has made many marvellous films.
Mi película favorita es … . Se trata de un hombre llamado … y una mujer llamada … .	My favourite film is … . It is about a man called … and a woman called … .
Ha ganado muchas medallas.	He/She has won lots of medals.
Ha ganado muchos premios/ muchos trofeos.	He/She has won many prizes/trophies.
Ha ayudado a los pobres.	He/She has helped the poor.
Trabajó toda su vida en …	He/She worked all his/her life in …
Ha jugado setenta veces con Inglaterra.	He/She has played seventy times for England.

Su personalidad

Es una persona amable/ generosa/muy dotada/ paciente/graciosa.	He/She is a pleasant/generous/very gifted/patient/funny person.
animado/a	lively
interesante	interesting
divertido/a	amusing
Ha hecho muchas cosas interesantes.	He/She has done many interesting things.
Ha ayudado a mucha gente.	He/She has helped many people.

Examiner's comments

Find a photo of the person doing something eye-catching and use it in your presentation.

Use the Internet to get information on your famous person.

Sample controlled assessment

Writing

1. Write about the advantages and disadvantages of modern technology. You could include...

- your views on mobile phones
- your views on the Internet
- the disadvantages of ICT
- how the Internet can affect your education.

Lo que me gusta más[16] es la seguridad que te[32] da un móvil. Es la cosa más útil del mundo.[23] Mis padres acaban de regalarme[20] el móvil que me habían prometido.[17] ¡Qué suerte tengo![1/9] Nunca[24] estás solo/a si tienes un móvil y puedes llamar a la policía fácilmente si necesitas. Antes de salir,[6] siempre digo a mis padres que me pueden llamar cuando quieran.[25] Se preocupan menos. Al hacer[7] mis deberes, con mi móvil nuevo puedo navegar por Internet para solucionar[31] dudas. Para divertirme,[31] mando e-mails, descargo videoclips y me divierto con los juegos. No hace ruido y tiene una cámara de cinco megapixels que puedo usar en el caso de un accidente o un crimen.

Tenemos Internet en mi instituto. Es magnífico. Es una manera excelente de comunicarse con amigos y desconocidos de todo el mundo. Además[16] me[32] permite usar y practicar lenguas extranjeras. Además, Internet ofrece grandes ventajas para hacer nuevas amistades. Me encanta la música y tengo un MP3 que es verdaderamente ligero[18] con una pantalla táctil.

Pero me doy cuenta[16] de que hay desventajas. Demasiada gente pasa demasiado tiempo delante del ordenador. Hacen menos deporte y después de pasar[8] tanto tiempo mirando la pantalla tienen problemas de vista. No se interesan en nada salvo su ordenador. Tienen ganas[1] de comer comida rápida delante de sus ordenadores. Se vuelven solitarios[16] y tristes y pierden a sus amigos. ¡Qué desastre![9] Para ayudar[31] a estas personas hay que limitar el acceso a Internet. Los móviles son peligrosos para la salud, dicen algunos expertos, por la radiación. Los científicos no están seguros. ¡Ten cuidado![9] Los jóvenes, sin escuchar[5] a sus profesores, envían SMSs durante sus clases. Tengo una amiga que está en contacto con un desconocido desde hace mucho tiempo.[26] ¡Qué mala idea![16] Necesito mi móvil, no puedo vivir sin él. Sin él, la vida sería[14] verdaderamente difícil[18] pero a fin de mes la factura es extremadamente cara.[18]

Turn to page 155 for a translation of this passage.

Turn to page 155 for a translation of this passage.

Examiner's comments

This piece of work, which includes a number of the 32 points on pages 8–9, is of A* quality:

1. 'Tener' structures
5. 'Sin' + the infinitive
6. 'Antes de...'
7. 'Al' + the infinitive
8. 'Después de' + the infinitive
9. Exclamations
14. An example of the conditional
16. Impressive vocabulary and structures, e.g. 'además', 'qué mala idea!'
17. An example of the pluperfect
18. 'Verdaderamente' and 'extremadamente' are alternatives to 'muy'
20. 'Acabar de'
23. An example of the superlative
24. A negative has been included
25. A subjunctive has been used
26. A 'desde hace' structure
31. Three examples of 'para' + the infinitive
32. Pronouns have been used

Exam practice questions

Listening

1 **Track 15** Three Spaniards explain why they do not have any free time. Tick the correct boxes.

(a) Alfonso is a person who…

A	likes to have a good time	☐	**C** is charitable	☐
B	dedicates himself to his studies	☐	**D** is lazy	☐

(b) Jaime is a person who…

A	likes to have a good time	☐	**C** is charitable	☐
B	dedicates himself to his studies	☐	**D** is lazy	☐

(c) Ana is a person who…

A	likes to have a good time	☐	**C** is charitable	☐
B	dedicates herself to her studies	☐	**D** is lazy	☐

(3)

2 **Track 16** Listen to Pablo, then tick the correct boxes.

(a) Pablo and Conchita…

    A met at university ☐   **B** were colleagues ☐   **C** were classmates ☐   **(1)**

(b) Pablo's mother is a…

    A cook ☐   **B** teacher ☐   **C** waitress ☐   **(1)**

(c) Choose three of the activities that Conchita and Pablo are going to do together.

A   D

☐   ☐

B   E

☐   ☐

C   F

☐   ☐   **(3)**

Exam practice questions

3 **Track 17** Carla and Fernando discuss film types. Write the name of the person in the correct boxes.

Film	Likes a lot	Likes a little	Does not like at all
Horror			
Westerns			
Romantic			
Adventure			

(8)

4 **Track 18** Someone is telling you about sport in Lima.

(a) What is the most popular sport?

....

(b) Why is the level of golf so high?

....

(c) Why is the city-centre pool famous?

....

(d) New York hosted a competition for which sport?

....

(e) What did the Peruvian team win?

....

(5)

5 **Track 19** Listen to this cinema's automatic answering machine. Tick the correct boxes.

		True	False
(a)	*Corazón de acero* is showing for three days.	☐	☐
(b)	*Corazón de acero* is a romantic film.	☐	☐
(c)	*Corazón de acero* is subtitled.	☐	☐
(d)	*Los muertos* is a horror film.	☐	☐
(e)	They are showing *Los muertos* for a week.	☐	☐
(f)	*Los muertos* is set in Great Britain.	☐	☐
(g)	*No me toques* is a comedy film.	☐	☐
(h)	*No me toques* has not won a prize.	☐	☐
(i)	Each film is shown three times a day.	☐	☐
(j)	The last showing is at midnight.	☐	☐

(10)

Exam practice questions

6 **Track 20** You are in the Corte Inglés. Tick the correct box for each question.

(a) Which floor for blouses?

A Third ☐

B Second ☐

C First ☐

D Basement ☐

(b) Which floor for suitcases?

A Third ☐

B Second ☐

C First ☐

D Basement ☐

(c) Which floor for bananas?

A Third ☐

B Second ☐

C First ☐

D Basement ☐

(d) Which floor for ties?

A Third ☐

B Second ☐

C First ☐

D Basement ☐ **(4)**

7 **Track 21** Listen to these people selling things in the market. Complete each sentence by choosing the correct words from the options given in the box below.

gratuito niños relojes paredes bueno superior baratos baratas legumbres
armas coches buena muebles

El primer puesto vende **(a)** ………………… y el vendedor dice que sus productos son los más

(b) ………………… del mercado.

El segundo puesto vende cosas para **(c)** ………………… y la vendedora menciona la calidad

(d) ………………… de sus productos.

El tercer puesto vende **(e)** ………………… y el vendedor dice que ofrece un servicio **(f)** …………………

de transporte. **(6)**

Exam practice questions

Reading

1 Read this extract from an e-mail and answer the questions that follow, ticking the correct boxes as required.

Al entrar en casa de Miguel sobre las siete ¡qué ambiente! ¡Cuánta gente! Todos mis amigos y todas mis amigas estaban allí ... todos se reían y cada uno me traía un regalo. Incluso había un pastel en forma de dieciocho con dieciocho velas encendidas. ¡Me lo pasé bomba! Luego sobre las nueve de la noche, ocurrió una cosa rara. Alguien llamó a la puerta, un amigo abrió y entró mi hermano. No pude dar crédito a mis ojos. Le vi por última vez hace tres años. Se marchó a Méjico y dijo que no volvería nunca. Por eso, nos abrazamos y los dos llorábamos. Pero él no fue el último visitante. Sobre las once hubo una llamada a la puerta. ¡Fue la Guardia Civil! Entraron y todos teníamos miedo. Los vecinos nos habían denunciado por el ruido. Nos amenazaron con multas pero al fin se fueron. Por eso, bajamos la música y a las doce mis amigos empezaron a marcharse. Mi hermana tuvo que irse a la cama. Estaba borracha, como es costumbre en ella. Fue una noche inolvidable. En mi próximo e-mail te contaré lo enfadado que estaba mi padre al ver la casa al día siguiente.

Con cariño

Laura

(a) What occasion were Laura and her friends celebrating?

....

(b) What was the atmosphere like in the house at seven o'clock?

   A   Sad   ☐

   B   Optimistic   ☐

   C   Happy   ☐

   D   Fearful   ☐

(c) How did Laura feel when her brother arrived?

   A   Disappointed   ☐

   B   Surprised   ☐

   C   Fearful   ☐

   D   Pessimistic   ☐

(d) How did people feel at nine o'clock when there was another visit?

   A   Disappointed   ☐

   B   Fearful   ☐

   C   Happy   ☐

   D   Optimistic   ☐

Exam practice questions

(e) How did the neighbours feel?

    A   Irritated   ☐

    B   Happy   ☐

    C   Fearful   ☐

    D   Pessimistic   ☐

(f) What does Laura's sister normally do?

    A   Drink too much   ☐

    B   Make too much noise   ☐

    C   Turn down the music   ☐

    D   Run away   ☐

(g) How did Laura's father feel?

    A   Happy   ☐

    B   Sad   ☐

    C   Proud   ☐

    D   Angry   ☐   **(7)**

2 Read this interview with Michael, of The Greens, and answer the questions that follow.

> Tiene 35 años y es famoso en todo el mundo. Pero el cantante del grupo irlandés The Greens propone utilizar sus melodías para plantear preguntas. Después de comer un poco y vestirse de negro Michael llega para empezar la entrevista.
>
> Para ti, ¿qué significa la música que haces? El éxito de la música significa muy poco. Para mí, cantar es como pintar. ¿Qué es una canción? Es como un cuadro.
>
> ¿Es difícil crear un buen grupo? Claro. Es muy difícil mantener al grupo unido puedes imaginar, aunque somos buenos amigos. Nos conocemos desde la edad de 14 años.
>
> ¿Cuál es el mensaje principal de tus canciones? Pues, cantando, podemos denunciar las injusticias del mundo. Aunque el rock no da respuestas. Plantea cuestiones.
>
> ¿Eres optimista pensando en el futuro? Personalmente, sí. He tenido suerte.

(a) What is Michael's role within the band? ....

(b) Where is the band from? ....

(c) For Michael, what is a song like? ....

(d) When did the band meet up? ....

(e) What does each song try to do? .... **(5)**

4 Holidays

The following topics are covered in this chapter:

- **Holidays and accommodation**
- **Transport**
- **Grammar**

4.1 Holidays and accommodation

LEARNING SUMMARY

After studying this section, you should be able to:

- talk about past and future holidays
- understand information about booking holidays and booking accommodation
- write about experiences abroad

Holidays and accommodation

AQA	✓
OCR	✓
EDEXCEL	✓
WJEC	✓
CCEA	✓

The holiday topic is the topic that lends itself to different tenses. It is the favourite topic for many students in the speaking and writing controlled assessments. The vocabulary sections are particularly important because they are very likely to be tested in the listening and reading exams.

Your controlled speaking assessment must last between four and six minutes. It is a long time to talk about one topic, so why not put two topics together? Your title could be 'The things I like doing'. You could spend two or three minutes speaking about your holidays and two or three minutes speaking about your hobbies (refer to Chapter 3 – Leisure, free time and the media).

On holiday (De vacaciones)

el turista

el alojamiento – lodgings
el alquiler – rent
la cámara – camera
la crema bronceadora – suncream
el descanso – rest
la dificultad – difficulty
el disgusto – annoyance, bother
la distracción – entertainment
el documento – document
la estancia – stay
la excursión – trip

los gastos – expenses
la información – information
el mapa – map
la máquina de fotos – camera
la mochila – rucksack
el regalo – present
el regreso – return
la postal – postcard
el trayecto – journey
el/la turista – tourist
el/la veraneante – holidaymaker

el saco de dormir

Camping (El camping)

el abrebotellas – bottle opener	**el gas** – gas
el abrelatas – tin opener	**la hoguera de campamento** – campfire
los aseos – toilets	**la pila** – battery
el camping – campsite	**el saco de dormir** – sleeping bag
el/la campista – camper	**la sala de juegos** – games room
la caravana – caravan	**el sitio** – place, spot
la cerilla – match	**la tienda** – shop
el espacio – space, pitch	**la tienda de campaña** – tent

At a hotel (En un hotel)

el equipaje

el ascensor – lift	**el nombre (de pila)** – (first) name
con vistas a – with a view of	**el país de origen** – country of origin
el/la dueño/a – owner	**el pasaporte** – passport
el equipaje – luggage	**la pensión** – boarding house
la ficha – form	**la pensión completa** – full board
la firma – signature	**el portero** – hotel porter
la habitación – room	**prohibida la entrada** – no entry
la habitación doble – double room	**el/la propietario/a** – owner
la habitación individual – single room	**la queja** – complaint
la habitación sencilla – single room	**la recepción** – reception
la hoja – form	**el/la recepcionista** – receptionist
el hotelero – hotel owner	**el retrete** – toilet
la llave – key	**la salida** – exit
el lujo – luxury	**las señas** – address
la media pensión – half board	**los servicios** – toilets
la nacionalidad – nationality	**la vista** – view

At the seaside (A orillas del mar)

la arena – sand	**el chalet** – villa	**el parasol** – parasol
la barca de pesca – fishing boat	**la costa** – coast	**la playa** – beach
	el mar – sea	**el puerto** – port
el barco – boat	**la ola** – wave	

Conversation

AQA ✓
OCR ✓
EDEXCEL ✓
WJEC ✓
CCEA ✓

¿Adónde fuiste de vacaciones el año pasado?

Fui a España.

¿Has visitado otros países?

He visitado Francia y Alemania.

¿Con quién fuiste?

Fui con mi familia.

¿Cómo fuiste?

Fui en avión/en barco/en coche.

¿Has visitado España?

Sí, visité España el año pasado.

¿Dónde te alojaste?

Me alojé en un hotel.

- ¿Cuánto tiempo estuviste en España?
- Estuve en España dos semanas.
- ¿Qué tiempo hizo?
- Hizo sol todos los días.
- ¿Qué hiciste allí?
- Tomé el sol y nadé en el mar.
- ¿Adónde irás este verano?
- Iré a España otra vez.

PROGRESS CHECK

Say or write the following in Spanish:

1. Double room
2. Beach

1. La habitación doble 2. La playa

4.2 Transport

LEARNING SUMMARY

After studying this section, you should be able to:

- take part in controlled speaking and writing assessments about transport
- answer listening and reading questions about how to get to places

Travel

AQA ✓
OCR ✓
EDEXCEL ✓
WJEC ✓
CCEA ✓

Transport (El transporte)

el horario

la aduana – customs	**el folleto** – brochure
el aeropuerto – airport	**la frontera** – border
la agencia de viajes – travel agent	**el gas-oil** – diesel oil
el asiento – seat	**el/la guía** – guide
la autopista – motorway	**la guía** – guidebook
el autostop – hitchhiking	**el horario** – timetable
el billete – ticket	**la huelga** – strike
el billete de ida – single ticket	**la línea aérea** – airline
el billete de ida y vuelta – return ticket	**la llegada** – arrival
la bolsa – bag	**la maleta** – suitcase
el canal – canal	**el metro** – underground train
la carretera – road	**las obras** – roadworks
el cruce – road junction	**el peaje** – motorway toll
la curva peligrosa – dangerous bend	**la reserva** – reservation
la demora – delay	**el retraso** – delay
con destino a – heading for	**las vacaciones** – holidays
la estación de autobuses – bus station	**la velocidad** – speed
	el viaje – journey
la estación de servicio – service station	**el/la viajero/a** – traveller
	el vuelo – flight
el extranjero – abroad	**la vuelta** – return

la azafata

People (La gente)

el/la **aduanero/a** – customs officer
el/la **autostopista** – hitchhiker
el/la **azafato/a** – flight attendant
el/la **cobrador(a)** – conductor
el/la **fumador(a)** – smoker

el/la **garajista** – garage attendant
el/la **habitante** – inhabitant
el/la **pasajero/a** – passenger
el/la **revisor(a)** – ticket inspector

Vehicles (Los vehículos)

el **autobús** – bus
el **autocar** – coach
el **avión** – plane
el **camión** – lorry
el **coche** – car

el **ferry** – ferry
el **helicóptero** – helicopter
la **moto** – motorcycle
el **taxi** – taxi
el **tranvía** – tram

By car (En coche)

el embotellamiento

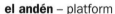

el **aceite** – oil
el **asiento** – seat
el **auto** – car
la **avería** – breakdown
la **batería** – battery
el **carnet de conducir** – driving licence
el **cinturón de seguridad** – safety belt
el **depósito** – fuel tank
el **desvío** – detour
el **embotellamiento** – traffic jam
el **faro** – headlight
los **frenos** – brakes
la **gasolina** – petrol
la **gasolinera** – petrol station
el **limpiaparabrisas** –
    windscreen wipers

el **maletero** – boot
el **mapa de carreteras** – road map
la **marca** – make
el/la **mecánico/a** – mechanic
el **modelo** – model
el **motor** – engine
el **neumático** – tyre
el **parabrisas** – windscreen
el **permiso de conducir** –
    driving licence
el **pinchazo** – puncture
la **reparación** – repair
la **rueda** – wheel
sin **plomo** – unleaded
la **velocidad** – speed

By train (En tren)

el mozo

el **andén** – platform
el **asiento** – seat
el **billete sencillo** – single ticket
el **coche cama** – sleeping car
el **coche restaurante** – dining car
la **consigna** – left-luggage office
el **departamento** – compartment
el **despacho de billetes** – ticket office
la **estación** – station
la **estación del ferrocarril** –
    railway station
el **mozo** – porter
la **primera clase** – first class

procedente de – coming from
la **red** – rack (in train), network
RENFE – Spanish Railways
la **sala de espera** – waiting room
la **segunda clase** – second class
el **suplemento** – supplement
Talgo – luxury, high-speed train
la **taquilla** – ticket office
el **transbordo** – connection
el **tren** – train
el **tren expreso** – express train
la **vía** – track

Europa

Francia

Portugal

España

Countries and nationalities
(Los países y las nacionalidades)

Alemania (f) – Germany
América del Sur (f) – South America
Argentina (f) – Argentina
Australia (f) – Australia
Austria (f) – Austria
Bélgica (f) – Belgium
Canadá (m) – Canada
Chile (m) – Chile
Dinamarca (f) – Denmark
Escocia (f) – Scotland
España (f) – Spain
los Estados Unidos – USA
Europa (f) – Europe
Francia (f) – France
Gales (m) – Wales
Gran Bretaña (f) – Great Britain
Grecia (f) – Greece
Holanda (f) – Holland
Inglaterra (f) – England
Irlanda (f) – Ireland
Irlanda del Norte (f) – Northern Ireland
Italia (f) – Italy
Japón (m) – Japan
Luxemburgo (m) – Luxembourg

Marruecos (m) – Morocco
Méjico, México (m) – Mexico
País de Gales (m) – Wales
Perú (m) – Peru
Portugal (m) – Portugal
el Reino Unido – United Kingdom
Rusia (f) – Russia
Suecia (f) – Sweden
Suiza (f) – Switzerland
Venezuela (f) – Venezuela

alemán (-ana) – German
americano/a – American
argentino/a – Argentinian
australiano/a – Australian
austríaco/a – Austrian
belga – Belgian
británico/a – British
canadiense – Canadian
chileno/a – Chilean
dinamarqués (-esa) – Danish
escocés (-esa) – Scottish
español(a) – Spanish
estadounidense – American

europeo/a – European
extranjero/a – foreigner
francés (-esa) – French
galés (-esa) – Welsh
griego/a – Greek
holandés (-esa) – Dutch
inglés (-esa) – English
irlandés (-esa) – Irish
italiano/a – Italian
japonés (-esa) – Japanese
luxemburgués (-esa) – of Luxembourg
marrueco/a, marroquí – Moroccan
mejicano/a, mexicano/a – Mexican
norteamericano/a – North American
peruano/a – Peruvian
portugués (-esa) – Portuguese
ruso/a – Russian
sudamericano/a – South American
sueco/a – Swedish
suizo/a – Swiss
venezolano/a – Venezuelan

Verbs

hacer las maletas

acampar – to camp
ahorrar – to save
alojarse – to stay (e.g. in a hotel)
alquilar – to hire
aparcar – to park
averiarse – to break down
bañarse – to bathe
broncearse – to get a tan, to sunbathe
coger una insolación – to get sunstroke
comprobar – to check
conducir – to drive
detenerse – to stop
dormir – to sleep
durar – to last
embarcarse – to embark

entrar – to enter
esperar – to wait, to hope, to expect
estacionar – to park
firmar – to sign
frenar – to brake
gastar – to spend (money)
hacer camping – to go camping
hacer las maletas – to pack
informarse – to find out
ir de camping – to go camping
ir de pesca – to go fishing
ir de vacaciones – to go on holiday
llegar – to arrive

llegar tarde – to be late
llenar – to fill (e.g. the fuel tank)
nadar – to swim
pasar – to spend (time), to happen
quedarse – to stay
rellenar un formulario – to fill in a form
reservar – to book
sacar fotos – to take photos
tomar el sol – to sunbathe
transbordar – to change trains
viajar – to travel
volar – to fly

Conversation

AQA ✓
OCR ✓
EDEXCEL ✓
WJEC ✓
CCEA ✓

¿Adónde fuiste de vacaciones el año pasado?¿Qué hiciste allí?

El año pasado fui a España con mi familia. ¡Lo pasé bomba![1] Comí muchísimo, bebí muchísimo, salí con mis amigos, bailé mucho y tomé[2] el sol. Me encanta España.[3]

¿Qué tiempo hizo?

Casi todos los días hizo buen tiempo. Hizo sol y calor. Sin embargo, un día llovió a cántaros[4] y nos mojamos hasta los huesos.[5]

¿Cómo viajaste a España?

Fuimos en coche al aeropuerto, tomamos el avión y al llegar[6] tomamos un taxi al hotel.

¿Adónde irás de vacaciones este año?

Iré otra vez a España con mi familia.

¿Qué harás allí?[7]

¡Lo pasaré bomba! Comeré muchísimo, beberé muchísimo, saldré con mis amigos, bailaré mucho y tomaré el sol.

¿Cómo viajarás a España?

Iré en coche al aeropuerto, tomaré el avión y al llegar tomaré un taxi al hotel.

1 'Pasarlo bomba' is a good expression for 'to have a great time'. Use it!

2 Some excellent preterite use here, but only one irregular preterite.

3 'Me encanta España' means 'I love Spain'. You have given an opinion, so you get extra marks.

4 'Llover a cántaros' means 'to pour with rain'. You could also say 'llover a chorros'.

5 'Nos mojamos hasta los huesos' means 'we got soaked to the skin'. The Spanish say 'soaked to the bones'.

6 'Al llegar' means 'on arriving' – a useful, mark-winning phrase.

7 Your chance to show your command of the future tense (see pages 123–124).

KEY POINT

Most of these questions are very predictable, so make sure you prepare for each one.

PROGRESS CHECK

Say or write the following in Spanish:

1 A postcard
2 A battery
3 A signature
4 To get sunstroke
5 The coast
6 Customs
7 A lorry
8 A breakdown
9 A station platform
10 Germany
11 German
12 I want to buy a postcard.
13 My sister has sunstroke.
14 Our car has broken down.
15 Which platform?
16 He is German.

1. Una postal 2. Una pila 3. Una firma 4. Coger una insolación 5. La costa 6. La aduana 7. Un camión 8. Una avería 9. Un andén 10. Alemania 11. Alemán 12. Quiero comprar una postal. 13. Mi hermana ha cogido una insolación. 14. Tenemos una avería. 15. ¿Qué andén? 16. Es alemán.

4.3 Grammar

After studying this section, you should be able to understand:

- the preterite tense
- negatives

The preterite tense

AQA	✓
OCR	✓
EDEXCEL	✓
WJEC	✓
CCEA	✓

KEY POINT

The preterite tense is sometimes known as the simple past. It is used to talk about events in the past, e.g. 'I went', 'you ran', 'they bought'.

The table below shows the preterite of three regular verbs. Note that there are two sets of endings, one for **-ar** verbs and one for **-er** and **-ir** verbs.

hablar		comer		vivir	
hablé	I spoke	**comí**	I ate	**viví**	I lived
hablaste	you spoke	**comiste**	you ate	**viviste**	you lived
habló	he/she/you spoke	**comió**	he/she/you ate	**vivió**	he/she/you lived
hablamos	we spoke	**comimos**	we ate	**vivimos**	we lived
hablasteis	you spoke	**comisteis**	you ate	**vivisteis**	you lived
hablaron	they/you spoke	**comieron**	they/you ate	**vivieron**	they/you lived

KEY POINT

Note the role played in English by 'did' in the negative and question forms of the preterite, e.g.:

hablé	I spoke
no hablé	I did not speak
¿Hablé?	Did I speak?

Radical-changing verbs in the preterite

KEY POINT

There are no **-ar** or **-er** radical-changing verbs in the preterite tense.
Some **-ir** verbs change **-e** to **-i** in the third-person singular and plural.

sonreír

pedir (to ask for)	
pedí	**pedimos**
pediste	**pedisteis**
pidió	**pidieron**
Other verbs like this are:		
preferir (to prefer)	**sentir** (to feel)	**vestirse** (to get dressed)
seguir (to follow)	**sonreír** (to smile)	**reír** (to laugh)

Spelling changes in the preterite

Note what happens to the first-person singular of verbs that end in **-zar**, **-gar** and **-car**.

empezar (to start)	➡	**empecé** (I started)
jugar (to play)	➡	**jugué** (I played)
buscar (to look for)	➡	**busqué** (I looked for)

You should also learn the preterite of **caer** (to fall).

caí	caímos
caíste	caísteis
cayó	cayeron

Irregular preterites

Here are some irregular preterites. Remember that **ser** and **ir** have the same preterite.

dar (to give)		**ser** (to be)/**ir** (to go)	
di	dimos	fui	fuimos
diste	disteis	fuiste	fuisteis
dio	dieron	fue	fueron

The pretérito grave

The pretérito grave is a particular kind of irregular preterite. The stress in the first and third-persons singular does not fall on the last syllable as it usually does, but on the second to last.

andar

andar (to walk)	**haber** (to have)	**querer** (to want)	**traer** (to bring)
anduve	hube	quise	traje
anduviste	hubiste	quisiste	trajiste
anduvo	hubo	quiso	trajo
anduvimos	hubimos	quisimos	trajimos
anduvisteis	hubisteis	quisisteis	trajisteis
anduvieron	hubieron	quisieron	trajeron

decir (to say)	**hacer** (to do/make)	**saber** (to know)	**venir** (to come)
dije	hice	supe	vine
dijiste	hiciste	supiste	viniste
dijo	hizo	supo	vino
dijimos	hicimos	supimos	vinimos
dijisteis	hicisteis	supisteis	vinisteis
dijeron	hicieron	supieron	vinieron

estar (to be)	**poder** (to be able)	**tener** (to have)	
estuve	pude	tuve	
estuviste	pudiste	tuviste	
estuvo	pudo	tuvo	
estuvimos	pudimos	tuvimos	
estuvisteis	pudisteis	tuvisteis	
estuvieron	pudieron	tuvieron	

PROGRESS CHECK

PROGRESS CHECK

Say or write the following in Spanish:

1. I spoke
2. I ate
3. I lived
4. He asked for
5. I played
6. I looked for
7. I fell
8. I gave
9. I was
10. I went

11. I walked
12. I wanted
13. I brought
14. I said
15. I made
16. I knew
17. I came
18. I could
19. I had
20. He came

1. Hablé 2. Comí 3. Viví 4. Pidió 5. Jugué 6. Busqué 7. Cayó 8. Di 9. Fui/estuve 10. Fui 11. Anduve 12. Quise 13. Traje 14. Dije 15. Hice 16. Supe 17. Vine 18. Pude 19. Tuve/hube 20. Vino

Negatives

AQA ✓
OCR ✓
EDEXCEL ✓
WJEC ✓
CCEA ✓

Learn these negative expressions.

nadie	nobody/no one
nada	nothing
nunca	never
jamás	never
ninguno/a	no
ni ... ni ...	neither ... nor ...
tampoco	(n)either

No hay nadie en la calle.	There is nobody in the street.
No hay nada en la calle.	There is nothing in the street.
No voy nunca/No voy jamás.	I never go.
No hay ningún trabajo allí.	There is no work there.
Ni mi amigo ni yo lo vimos.	Neither my friend nor I saw it.
No fui y ella tampoco fue.	I didn't go and she didn't go either.

KEY POINT

When the negative word comes after the verb, **no** must be placed before the verb:

Nunca voy a la iglesia.	I never go to church.
No voy nunca al colegio.	I never go to school.

PROGRESS CHECK

Say or write the following in Spanish:

1. Nobody
2. Nothing
3. Never
4. Neither ... nor ...
5. No

1. Nadie 2. Nada 3. Nunca/jamás 4. Ni ... ni ... 5. Ninguno/a

Sample controlled assessment

Speaking

1 You are discussing last year's holiday with a Spanish friend. Your teacher will play the part of the friend. You will be asked about the following:

- What you did for your holidays last year
- What the weather was like
- What the journey to your holiday destination was like
- Your overall impressions
- **?** An unprepared question (e.g. your holiday plans for next year).

Student: El año pasado, decidí ir[4] de vacaciones en junio con mi hermano mayor.[16] Quería visitar[13] a mis amigos en Suiza. Viven allí desde hace dos años.[26] ¡Qué buena idea![9] Creo que Suiza es el país más bonito del mundo porque las montañas son fantásticas.[3]

Teacher: ¿Qué tiempo hacía?

Student: Hacía buen tiempo y fuimos al aeropuerto en taxi. Subimos en el avión y encontré un sitio. Me abroché el cinturón y el avión despegó. No tenía miedo.[1]

Teacher: ¿Qué hiciste durante el vuelo?

Student: Antes de coger[6] el avión, había comprado[17] una novela. Jugué a las cartas y leí. Comimos pero la comida no era buena. Comimos pollo pero no me gustó. Después de comer,[8] me sentía enfermo/a.[13] Llegué a Suiza a las seis y mis amigos me esperaban en el aeropuerto. Eran muy simpáticos. Atraversamos la ciudad de Ginebra, admiramos el lago, luego llegamos a la casa. Al llegar,[7] comimos una cena excelente y nos acostamos.

Teacher: ¿Tus impresiones?

Student: El viaje fue muy agradable y mis amigos eran muy simpáticos.

Teacher: Y ¿el año que viene?

Student: Mis amigos me dijeron que volviese[25] a Suiza para esquiar.[31] Me gustaría esquiar porque[2] me gusta mucho y la nieve es tan buena[18] en Verbier. También me gustaría montar a caballo porque[2] tengo un caballo aquí en Inglaterra y me gusta hacer equitación a pesar del tiempo.[19] El año pasado di unos paseos por la montaña y me gustaría hacer igual puesto que[30] me gustó mucho. También hay una pista de patinaje y una piscina en Verbier.

Turn to page 156 for a translation of this passage.

Examiner's comments

This student has boosted his/her grade by including a number of the 32 mark-winning points outlined on pages 8–9:

1	A 'tener' structure
2	Two examples of the use of 'porque'
3	A fine example of a justified point of view
4	'Decidí' + the infinitive
6	'Antes de…'
7	'Al' + the infinitive
8	'Después de' + the infinitive
9	An exclamation
13	Two examples of the imperfect
16	An impressive structure
17	An example of the pluperfect
18	'Tan' has been used here instead of 'muy'
19	An 'a pesar de' structure
25	The subjunctive has been used
26	A 'desde hace' structure
30	'Que' is a good connective
31	'Para' + the infinitive

Sample controlled assessment

2 You are going to have a conversation with your teacher about the series of pictures below, which outline a bicycle ride in Spain.

10:00 en bicicleta   11:00 en el café   12:00 problema

2:30   1:30   12:30

3:00   4:00

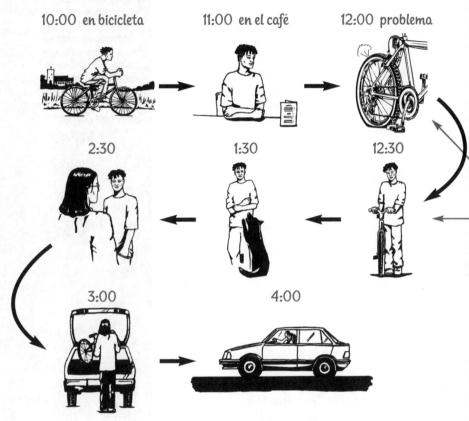

Track 23

Teacher:	¿Qué pasó?
Student:	Esta mañana, fui de paseo en bicicleta. Lo pasé bomba. Hacía sol y hacía calor. Llevaba mi jersey amarillo. Vi muchos edificios interesantes y visité una iglesia antigua. Bebí una limonada y comí un bocadillo en un café.
Teacher:	¿Qué pasó después?
Student:	Después de salir del café, decidí volver a casa. Desgraciadamente cinco minutos más tarde tuve un pinchazo. Estaba en el campo y no había nadie para ayudarme.
Teacher:	¡Qué mala suerte!
Student:	Empecé a andar con la bicicleta. Dos horas más tarde, estaba triste, tenía hambre y sed. Luego hubo un incidente. Un perro me atacó y tuve que huir. Más tarde encontré a un hombre muy simpático. El hombre me ayudó. Puso mi bicicleta en su coche y me llevó a casa.
Teacher:	¡Qué bien! ¿Cómo era el hombre?
Student:	Era bastante viejo, tenía los ojos azules y el pelo largo y negro. Llevaba gafas. Era muy simpático. ¡Qué día!

Examiner's comments

Your controlled speaking assessment on holidays might involve talking about a series of pictures, like the ones shown here. Be aware that the conversation must last at least four minutes, therefore you would need to add further detail to the model extract shown below left.

'Un pinchazo' is a puncture.

Try to invent detail.

You need to know the imperfect for descriptions.

Sample controlled assessment

3 You are going to have a conversation with your teacher about the series of pictures below, which outline an experience in Spain.

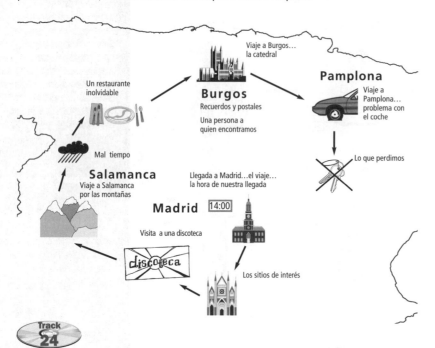

Examiner's comments

Your controlled speaking assessment on holidays might involve talking about a series of pictures, like the ones shown here. Be aware that the conversation must last at least four minutes, therefore you would need to add further detail to the model extract shown below left.

Track 24

Teacher: ¿Qué pasó?

Student: Después de viajar dos horas, llegué a Madrid en coche con mi familia a las dos de la tarde. Sin perder un momento, encontré un hotel y fui a visitar los sitios de interés. Visité la catedral y vi el palacio real. Más tarde fui a una discoteca y bailé y charlé con la gente.
Al día siguiente, viajé con mi familia en coche a Salamanca. Fuimos por las montañas y llovía a cántaros. ¡Estábamos mojados hasta los huesos! Fuimos a un restaurante inolvidable. Comí mariscos, una chuleta de cerdo con patatas, queso y fruta. Bebí agua mineral.

Teacher: ¿Qué pasó después?

Student: Al día siguiente, viajamos a Burgos. Visité la catedral y compré recuerdos y postales. También compré regalos para mis amigos en Inglaterra. Encontré a mi amigo por correspondencia en Burgos. Vive allí y fuimos al cine juntos.

Teacher: Fuiste a Pamplona, ¿no?

Student: Sí, pero cerca de Pamplona tuvimos un problema con el coche. Tuvimos un pinchazo y mi padre lo reparó. Pero más tarde perdió las llaves del coche. ¡Mi madre las encontró en su bolsillo! ¡Qué día!

Knowledge of the preterite is essential here.

Make sure you can describe a meal.

'Al día siguiente' means 'on the following day'. A very useful time description.

You will get extra marks if you can use a direct object pronoun like this one ('las').

Sample controlled assessment

Writing

1 Write about a recent holiday. You could include...

- the destination
- the accommodation
- who you went with
- your overall opinion
- your plans for this summer.

Voy a describirte mis vacaciones en Blackpool. Estaba en un hotel de cuatro estrellas. Era estupendo porque la piscina estaba siempre vacía. ¡Qué lujo!

Por la mañana, me paseaba por la playa: por la tarde, jugaba al fútbol en el parque y más tarde salía con mis padres. Un día fui a un parque de atracciones. Era horroroso porque las colas eran tan largas.

En mi opinión, las vacaciones eran excelentes porque lo pasamos muy bien todo el tiempo. Hacía buen tiempo todos los días.

En verano, iré a los Estados Unidos y veré todos los monumentos históricos. Me gustaría ver Nueva York.

Now compare the piece of work above with the following passage.

Voy a describirte[12/32] mi estancia en Blackpool. Acabo de pasar[20] dos semanas inolvidables.[15] Para mí, Blackpool es la mejor ciudad de Inglaterra para pasar las vacaciones porque siempre hay algo que hacer.[3] Estaba en un hotel de cinco estrellas porque[2] mis padres habían ganado[17] la lotería. ¡Era estupendo porque[2] la piscina estaba[13] siempre tan vacía![18] ¡Qué lujo![9] Ganaron una fortuna así que hemos comprado un coche excelente y nos hospedamos en los mejores hoteles.[16] Afortunadamente[16] mi hermana menor[16] se negó a acompañarnos[32] porque[2] no le gusta Blackpool. Ella fue a ver a mi abuela.

Por la mañana daba[13] paseos por la playa. Por la tarde jugaba[13] al fútbol en el parque y más tarde salía[13] con mis padres. Mis padres me dijeron que hiciese[25] mucho ejercicio para mantenerme[31] en buena condición física. Un día decidí ir[4] a un parque de atracciones. Al llegar,[7] vi las colas.[16] Era espantoso porque[2] las colas estaban tan largas.[18] Después de esperar[8] dos horas, no estaba contento/a. Estaba a punto de[21] pedir un reembolso. Nunca[24] volveré a estos parques.

En mi opinión las vacaciones fueron excelentes porque lo pasamos bien todo el tiempo y tuve la suerta de salir con una chica guapa/un chico guapo.[3] Salí con ella/él muchas veces y nos entendíamos muy bien. Hacía buen tiempo todos los días. Yo volvería allí[14] sin vacilar[5] a pesar de[19] las colas largas.

En verano, iré a los Estados Unidos y veré a mi hermano mayor.[16] Vive allí desde hace dos años.[26] Me gustaría ver Nueva York y él me acompañará. Tengo ganas de[1] cruzar el país para explorar. Mi hermano alquilará un coche y nos marchamos.

Turn to page 156 for a translation of this passage.

Turn to page 156 for a translation of this passage.

Examiner's comments

The first version is too short and has few mark-winning structures. It would not get a high grade. The second passage is about the right length and uses most of the 32 points on pages 8–9, making it worth an A*:

1. A 'tener' structure
2. Several uses of 'porque'
3. Two justified points of view
4. 'Decidí' + the infinitive
5. 'Sin' + the infinitive
7. 'Al' + the infinitive
8. 'Después de' + the infinitive
9. An exclamation
12. An example of the future tense
13. Numerous examples of the imperfect tense
14. An example of the conditional
15. An example of an adjective
16. Good vocabulary and structures, e.g. 'los mejores hoteles', 'afortunadamente', 'mi hermana menor', 'las colas'
17. An example of the pluperfect
18. Two examples of 'tan' being used
19. 'A pesar de'
20. An 'acabar de' structure
21. 'Estar a punto de'
24. A negative has been used
25. A subjunctive has been included. Excellent!
26. A 'desde hace' structure
31. 'Para' + the infinitive
32. Examples of pronouns

Sample controlled assessment

2 Look at this controlled writing assessment task. You see a prize being offered in a Spanish magazine. The prize is a trip around the world. Write an article addressing these points:

- When you read the magazine and why you like it.
- Why you want to travel.
- The person that will go with you.
- Where you will go and when.
- Why you deserve to win the prize.

Acabo de[20] comprar la revista y estoy seguro/a que es la mejor[23] revista que he leído.[16] La leí[11] en seguida. Me interesan los artículos sobre la moda y el deporte. También los artículos sobre los problemas de los jóvenes en España son interesantes.[3] Me gusta viajar porque[2] quiero conocer otros países del mundo y quiero hacer amigos en todas partes. Viajaría[14] con mi hermano y mi hermana porque[2] aparte de ser miembros de mi familia son mis mejores[15] amigos.

Los dos sitios que me interesan más son Nueva York, porque he visto[16] la ciudad muchas veces en la televisión, y Honolulu porque[2] me han dicho[16] que el clima allí es perfecto. Me gustaría[14] hacer el viaje durante las vacaciones de verano porque[2] quiero volver antes del cinco de septiembre.

Yo creo que[30] deberían[14] darme el premio porque nunca[24] he ido al extranjero. Mis padres son muy pobres y si no gano quizás nunca podré[12] ir al extranjero.

3 Write an e-mail to the tourist office in Málaga mentioning details of an imaginary visit there last year and why you wish to return.

Estimado Señor:
Soy[10] inglés/inglesa y pasé[11] unas semanas en Málaga el año pasado. Quiero[10] volver a Málaga este año. ¿Puede[10] Vd. encontrarme un hotel barato?[15]
Seremos cuatro: un amigo, mi hermano, mi hermana y yo. Buscamos cuatro habitaciones individuales y preferimos habitaciones con baño. Llegaremos[12] en avión el tres de junio y nos marcharemos[12] el diecisiete de junio.
Me encanta Málaga.[3] Me gustan las playas y las montañas cerca de la ciudad. Sobre todo me gusta el clima. El año pasado me quedé[11] en el Hotel Sol cerca del ayuntamiento.[16] No quiero volver[24] allí porque[2] era[13] demasiado ruidoso, había[13] insectos en la cama y creo que el dueño es un ladrón.[3]
Este año quiero hacer más excursiones para visitar[31] los lugares de interés cerca de la ciudad. Haga el favor de mandarme detalles de excursiones cerca de la ciudad.
Le saluda atentamente,
J. Parkinson

Examiner's comments

This example would be worth a good grade because it uses a number of the '32 points for improving your grade' from pages 8–9:

- 2 Examples of the use of 'porque'
- 3 An opinion has been given
- 11 An example of the preterite
- 12 An example of the future tense
- 14 Examples of the conditional
- 15 An adjective
- 16 Impressive structures (i.e. examples of the perfect tense)
- 20 'Acabar de'
- 23 A superlative has been included
- 24 A negative has been used
- 30 A connecting word

Examiner's comments

This good piece of work has a number of mark-winning features, which are again referenced to the '32 points for improving your grade' on pages 8–9:

- 2 'Porque'
- 3 Opinions are offered
- 10 Plenty of correct present tenses
- 11 Correct usage of the preterite tense
- 12 Future tenses have been used
- 13 Extra marks for using the imperfect
- 15 An adjective
- 16 Impressive vocabulary
- 24 A negative has been used
- 31 'Para' + the infinitive

Exam practice questions

Listening

1  A British tourist goes to the Lost Property Office in Barcelona.

Complete the gaps with the correct words.

(a) He lost his ....

(b) It is .... and quite big and contains money, ... and his passport.

(c) He lost it in the .... When? .... **(5)**

WJEC Foundation Tier

2  Listen to Fernando. Tick the correct boxes to answer each question.

(a) What is he looking for?

A 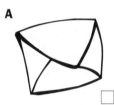 ☐   B ☐   C  ☐   D ☐

(b) What present does he buy?

A 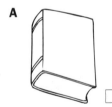 ☐   B 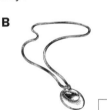 ☐   C  ☐   D 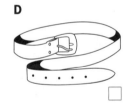 ☐

(c) Which sport does he prefer?

A  ☐   B  ☐   C 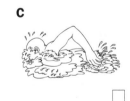 ☐   D 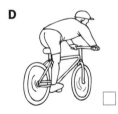 ☐

(d) Where is the money?

A 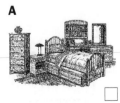 ☐   B  ☐   C 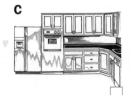 ☐   D  ☐

Exam practice questions

(e) What will they visit?

A   B   C   D

(f) Where is the book shop?

A   B   C   D

SOTANO   PRIMERA PLANTA   SEGUNDA PLANTA   TERCERA PLANTA

(g) When does the bus leave?

A   B   C   D

(h) How does Isabel travel?

A   B   C   D

(i) Where does Isabel want to go?

A   B   C   D

(j) When does Isabel return?

A   B   C   D

04:08   05:09   06:03   07:10

(10)

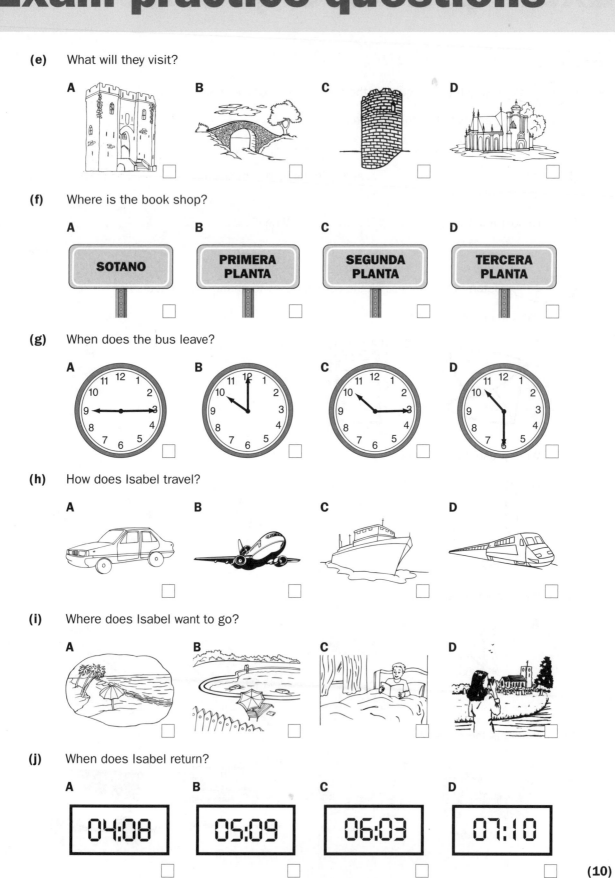

Exam practice questions

3 *Track 27* You are on a coach tour in Spain. The guide is talking to the people on the coach using a microphone. Tick the correct boxes.

(a) You will get to the hotel in...

　A　20 minutes　☐

　B　30 minutes　☐

　C　50 minutes　☐

　D　60 minutes　☐

(b) Before getting to the hotel, you are going to...

　A　stop to look at the cathedral　☐

　B　see the places of interest　☐

　C　see the cathedral　☐

　D　see a video　☐

(c) This evening you are going to...

　A　eat then watch a video　☐

　B　see a video then eat　☐

　C　see the places of interest　☐

　D　make a video　☐

(d) Tomorrow...

　A　the morning is free and in the afternoon you will visit the cathedral　☐

　B　the whole day is free　☐

　C　a trip is organised for the morning but nothing is organised for the afternoon　☐

　D　there are two trips organised　☐

(e) You will stay in Zaragoza...

　A　one day　☐

　B　two days　☐

　C　three days　☐

　D　four days　☐

(f) If you have a problem in the hotel you must...

　A　call the guide　☐

　B　go to reception　☐

　C　go to room three　☐

　D　call the hotel　☐

(6)

Exam practice questions

Reading

1 Read the e-mail below and then complete the sentences by choosing the correct word from the options given in the box.

> Saludos. Estoy pasando dos semanas aquí en la capital de Francia y hace sol y calor. Los franceses son muy simpáticos y nos encanta la cocina francesa. Disfrutamos tanto de nuestra estancia aquí que no queremos volver a España. Ayer tuvimos un pequeño problema con el coche: los frenos dejaron de funcionar.
>
> Hasta pronto
>
> Angela y familia

ganas	puente	bien	estupendo	libro	avería	quincena	París	cocina	gente
		barcos	jueves	día					

Angela y su familia pasan una **(a)** .... en **(b)** .... y el tiempo es **(c)** ....

Les gusta la **(d)** .... y la **(e)** .... No tienen **(f)** .... de volver a España

porque se lo pasan **(g)** .... en Francia. Ayer el coche tuvo una **(h)** .... Se trataba

de los frenos.   **(8)**

2 Here is a list of phone numbers.

TELEFONOS DE INTERES

Aeropuerto Información Iberia	32 20 00
Ayuntamiento	82 02 00
Bomberos	77 43 79
RENFE	31 25 00
Información de carreteras	81 21 20
Información meteorológica	34 24 40
Agencia de viajes	77 40 40
Noticias	31 32 30

Which number do you call if you...

(a) want to know the weather? ....

(b) have left your umbrella on the train? ....

(c) want to book a holiday? ....

(d) want information about a flight? ....

(e) want road traffic information? ....   **(5)**

Exam practice questions

3 At the hotel. Match the drawings with the requests.

A Buenos días. Necesito un televisor en mi habitación. Una habitación con dos camas individuales, por favor.

B Llegaré solo así que necesito una habitación con cama individual.

C No quiero baño. Necesito una habitación con ducha y una cama de matrimonio.

D Prefiero una habitación con baño. Somos tres. Necesito una cama de matrimonio y una cama individual.

Write the correct letter in the answer spaces.

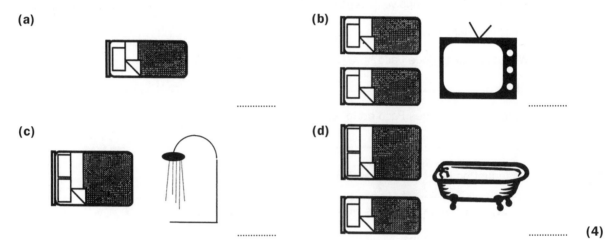

(a) ....

(b) ....

(c) ....

(d) .... **(4)**

4 Read this e-mail and then answer the questions that follow.

Hola Jason

Acabo de comprarme el billete de avión y ahora es segurísimo. Voy a ir a Escocia a principios de agosto. ¡Tengo un poco de miedo! No conozco Escocia y me dicen que los mosquitos son un problema en verano. Sobre todo en la costa oeste. Me gustaría viajar por todo el país pero sobre todo quiero visitar las islas.

Voy a visitar a mi amiga Sally: vive en Edinburgo. Tienen una casa bastante pequeña y lamentablemente tendré que compartir una habitación. Sally tiene un hermano que se llama Barry. Barry tiene coche y dice que podemos hacer excursiones para ver los lugares de interés. También tiene una hermana, Jane. Jane tiene un caballo y dice que va a enseñarme a montar a caballo. No me gusta esta idea porque no quiero caerme y hacerme daño. Pero si me enseñan un poco de inglés, estaré contento.

Para poder ir a Escocia, tengo que ahorrar y ganar dinero. Reparto periódicos y trabajo en el jardín de un vecino anciano. Jason ¿por qué no vienes conmigo?

Contesta pronto, Paco

(a) What has Paco just done? .... **(1)**

(b) Where is Paco going? .... **(1)**

(c) When in August is Paco travelling? .... **(1)**

(d) Give two reasons why Paco is apprehensive.

(i) .... **(ii)** .... **(2)**

Exam practice questions

(e) In what part of the country is there a problem? .... **(1)**

(f) What part of the country does Paco particularly want to visit? .... **(1)**

(g) What will Paco have to do in Sally's house? .... **(1)**

(h) What has Barry offered to do? .... **(1)**

(i) What has Jane offered to do? .... **(1)**

(j) Why is Paco apprehensive of Jane's offer? .... **(1)**

(k) What will make Paco happy? .... **(1)**

(l) What two things does Paco have to do in order to go on holiday?

    (i) .... **(ii)** .... **(2)**

(m) What two things does Paco do to earn money?

    (i) .... **(ii)** .... **(2)**

5 Read this leaflet on how to avoid travel sickness on an aeroplane.

¿Vas de vacaciones en avión? Unos consejos si no quieres marearte.

- Durante el viaje, no bebas alcohol.
- Échate una siesta durante el viaje.
- Come bien antes de despegar.
- Debes levantarte de vez en cuando a dar un paseo por el avión.
- Toma tus pastillas la víspera del viaje.
- No leas: escucha música.
- Paga lo que cuesta para ver las películas de abordo.
- Charla con la azafata.

Complete the sentences by choosing the correct words from the options given in the box below.

| te quedes | conversación | licores | lectura | anterior | dormir | vacío | caras |

Mientras viajas, evita **(a)** .... e intenta **(b)** ....

No debes despegar con el estómago **(c)** .... y durante el vuelo no **(d)**

.... en tu sitio todo el tiempo. Tómate las medicinas el día **(e)**

....

La **(f)** .... puede marearte. Escucha música en su lugar.

Las películas serán **(g)** .... pero es preferible pagar.

Entabla **(h)** .... con la tripulación. **(8)**

5 Home, local area and environment

The following topics are covered in this chapter:

- Special occasions celebrated in the home
- Home and local area
- The environment
- Grammar

5.1 Special occasions celebrated in the home

LEARNING SUMMARY

After studying this section, you should be able to:

- describe different special occasions
- say how you celebrate special occasions

Special occasions

AQA	✓
OCR	✓
EDEXCEL	✓
WJEC	✓
CCEA	✓

You need to study the vocabulary and know the Spanish for special occasions like Christmas and Easter. These may well appear in your reading and listening exams. You might have to describe a special occasion for your controlled writing or speaking assessment.

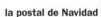
la postal de Navidad

Celebrations (Las celebraciones)

el año nuevo – New Year
el año nuevo chino – Chinese New Year
el árbol de Navidad – Christmas tree
la boda – wedding
el día de año nuevo – New Year's Day
el día de mi santo – Saint's day
el día de Navidad – Christmas Day
el Diwali – Diwali
el Eid – Eid
¡Feliz año nuevo! – Happy New Year!
¡Feliz cumpleaños! – Happy birthday!
¡Felices Navidades!, ¡Felices Pascuas! – Happy Christmas!

¡Feliz santo! – Happy saint's day!
el huevo de Pascua – Easter egg
el nacimiento – birth
la Navidad – Christmas
las Navidades – Christmas time
la Nochebuena – Christmas Eve
la Nochevieja – New Year's Eve
la Pascua – Easter
el Ramadán – Ramadan
¡Saludos! – Best wishes!
la Semana Santa – Holy Week
la postal de Navidad – Christmas card
la víspera de Navidad – Christmas Eve

Useful expressions

¡Enhorabuena!

de acuerdo – agreed	**¡Qué bien!** – How good!
¡Bienvenido/a! – Welcome!	**¡Qué horror!** – How terrible!
desde luego – of course	**¡Qué lástima!** – What a pity!
¡Enhorabuena! – Congratulations!	**¡Qué pena!** – What a pity!
me da igual – I don't mind	**lo siento** – I'm sorry
mucha suerte – good luck	**¡Socorro!** – Help!
mucho gusto – pleased to meet you	**¡Suerte!** – Good luck!
de nada – don't mention it	**¡Vale!** – OK!
¡Qué asco! – How disgusting!	**vale la pena** – it's worthwhile

Conversation starters

En navidades,	**mandamos...** — we send...
El día de año nuevo,	**damos...** — we give...
El día de mi cumpleaños,	**decoramos...** — we decorate...
El día de todos los santos,	**cantamos...** — we sing...
En Diwali,	**comemos...** — we eat...
Al final de Ramadán,	**celebramos...** — we celebrate...
En Hannoukah,	**ayunamos...** — we fast...
El día del año nuevo chino,	**bebemos...** — we drink...
	encendemos... — we light...
	decimos... — we say...
	bailamos... — we dance...

Useful phrases

Compramos regalos.
We buy presents.
Mandamos postales.
We send cards.
Decoramos la casa.
We decorate the house.
Comemos mucho.
We eat a lot.
Recibimos postales y regalos.
We get cards and presents.

Hay un desfile, un baile al aire libre y fuegos artificiales.
There is a procession, an open-air dance and fireworks.
Damos regalos.
We give presents.

Ponemos luces en el exterior de la casa.

We put up lights outside.

Comemos turrón.

We eat nougat.

Turrón is a nougat confection eaten as a traditional dessert at Christmas in Spain.

Encendemos velas.

We light candles.

Jugamos a juegos.

We play games.

Nos lo pasamos muy bien.

We have a good time.

Nos acostamos muy de madrugada.

We go to bed very late.

Say or write the following in Spanish:
1. Happy Christmas!
2. New Year's Day
3. We buy presents.
4. We play games.
5. They eat nougat.
6. We decorate the house.
7. There is a procession, an open-air dance and fireworks.

1. ¡Felices Navidades! 2. El día de año nuevo 3. Compramos regalos. 4. Jugamos a juegos. 5. Comen turrón. 6. Decoramos la casa. 7. Hay un desfile, un baile al aire libre y fuegos artificiales.

5.2 Home and local area

After studying this section, you should be able to:

- describe your home
- say what you do at home
- talk about your town, neighbourhood and region
- give and understand directions
- describe the weather and understand a weather forecast

Home

AQA	✓
OCR	✓
EDEXCEL	✗
WJEC	✓
CCEA	✓

The following vocabulary and sentences will help you in the listening and reading exams. In the controlled speaking assessment, you may be asked to talk for a minute or two about your home, describing the rooms and the garden. You need to be able to talk in the preterite tense about what you did at home and in the future tense about what you will do there. A popular choice for the controlled writing or speaking assessments is to describe your ideal home.

Houses (Las casas)

la casa adosada – semi-detached house
la casa de campo – country house

la casa de una planta, el bungalow – bungalow
la casa no adosada – detached house

Around the home (En casa)

la cortina

el aire aclimatizado – air conditioning
el aire acondicionado – air conditioning
el balcón – balcony
la bombilla – light bulb
la calefacción central – central heating
la casa – house
la cortina – curtain
el cristal – pane of glass
el cuadro – picture
el cubo de la basura – rubbish bin
la electricidad – electricity
la esquina – corner (outside)
la lámpara – lamp
la luz (las luces) – light(s)
los muebles – furniture

la papelera – wastepaper basket
la pared – wall
la persiana – blinds
la planta baja – the ground floor
el primer piso – first floor
la puerta – door, gate
la puerta principal – front door
el radiador – radiator
el reloj – clock
el rincón – corner (inside)
el suelo – floor
el techo – ceiling
el tejado – roof
la ventana – window

Rooms (Las habitaciones)

la escalera

el comedor – dining room
el cuarto de baño – bathroom
el cuarto de estar – living room
el dormitorio – bedroom
la escalera – stairs
el estudio – study
el garaje – garage

la habitación – room, bedroom
el pasillo – corridor
el patio – patio
la sala de estar – living room
el salón – living room
el sótano – basement
el vestíbulo – hall

Materials (Los materiales)

el acero – steel
el algodón – cotton
el cuero – leather
el hierro – iron
la lana – wool

la madera – wood
el nilón – nylon
el oro – gold
la piel – leather
la plata – silver

el plomo – lead
la seda – silk
el vidrio – glass

Adjectives

amueblado/a – furnished
cómodo/a – comfortable
ideal – ideal
importante – important
incómodo/a – uncomfortable
interior – interior

lujoso/a – luxurious
magnífico/a – magnificent
mismo/a – same
moderno/a – modern
otro/a – another
viejo/a – old

Verbs

cocinar

afeitarse – to shave	**funcionar** – to work (of machinery)
apagar – to switch off (e.g. light)	**lavar** – to wash
aparcar – to park	**lavar los platos** – to wash the dishes
barrer – to sweep	**lavarse** – to get washed
calentar – to heat	**lavarse el pelo** – to wash one's hair
casarse – to get married	**lavarse los dientes** – to clean
cepillarse – to brush (e.g. teeth, hair)	one's teeth
cerrar – to close	**levantarse** – to get up
cerrar con llave – to lock	**limpiar** – to clean
cocinar – to cook	**madrugar** – to get up early
coger – to get	**pasar la aspiradora** – to do
compartir – to share	the vacuuming
dejar – to let, to leave	**peinarse** – to comb one's hair
descansar – to rest	**planchar** – to iron
desnudarse – to get undressed	**poner la mesa** – to lay the table
despertarse – to wake up	**quitar la mesa** – to clear the table
dormir – to sleep	**reparar** – to repair
dormirse – to fall asleep	**secar** – to dry
ducharse – to have a shower	**vestirse** – to get dressed
encender la luz – to switch on the light	

Living room (La sala de estar)

la alfombra – carpet	**la cómoda** – chest	**la pintura** – painting
el aparador – sideboard	of drawers	**la radio** – radio
la butaca – armchair	**la estantería** – shelf	**el sillón** – armchair
el canapé – settee	**el estéreo** – stereo, hi-fi	**el sofá** – settee
la chimenea – fireplace	**la librería** – bookcase	**el televisor** – TV (set)
	la moqueta – carpet	**el vídeo** – video (recorder)

el despertador

Bedroom (El dormitorio)

la almohada – pillow	**el despertador** –	**el póster** – poster
el cajón – drawer	alarm clock	**la sábana** – sheet
la cama – bed	**el estante** – shelf	**la secadora/el secador**
la cama de matrimonio	**el guardarropa, el**	**de pelo** – hairdryer
– double bed	**armario** – wardrobe	**el tocador** – dressing
la cómoda – chest	**la manta** – blanket	table
of drawers	**el ordenador** – computer	

Bathroom (El cuarto de baño)

el baño – bath	**el jabón** – soap	**la pasta de dientes** –
el cepillo de dientes –	**el lavabo** – washbasin	toothpaste
toothbrush	**el maquillaje** – make-up	**el peine** – comb
el champú – shampoo	**la máquina de afeitar** –	**el perfume** – perfume
la ducha – shower	electric shaver	**las tijeras** – scissors
el espejo – mirror	**la maquinilla de afeitar**	**la toalla** – towel
el grifo – tap	– razor	

Kitchen (La cocina)

el microondas

el abrelatas – tin-opener
el armario – cupboard
la bandeja – tray
la cacerola – saucepan
la cocina – cooker
la cocina de gas – gas cooker
la cocina eléctrica – electric cooker
el congelador – freezer

el fregadero – sink
el frigorífico – fridge
el grifo – tap
el horno – oven
la lata – tin
la lavadora – washing machine
el lavaplatos – dishwasher
la mesa – table

el microondas – microwave oven
la nevera – fridge
el olor – smell
el sacacorchos – corkscrew
la sartén – frying pan
la silla – chair
la taza – cup

Garden (El jardín)

la aspiradora

el árbol – tree
el arbusto – shrub
el césped – lawn
la flor – flower
la hierba – grass

la hoja – leaf
el manzano – apple tree
el muro – wall
la planta – plant
la rama – branch

la rosa – rose
el sendero – path
el seto – hedge

Housework (Las tareas domésticas)

la aspiradora – vacuum cleaner
la basura – rubbish

el cepillo – brush
la mancha – stain
el orden – order (tidiness)

la plancha – iron
los quehaceres – chores

PROGRESS CHECK

Say or write the following in Spanish:
1. Dishwasher
2. Bedroom
3. Toothbrush
4. Bed
5. Yesterday I washed the dishes.
6. This evening I will cook the dinner.

1. El lavaplatos   2. El dormitorio/la habitación   3. El cepillo de dientes   4. La cama
5. Ayer lavé los platos.   6. Esta tarde prepararé la cena.

Conversation: Grades G–D

AQA	✓
OCR	✓
EDEXCEL	✗
WJEC	✓
CCEA	✓

You need to be able to answer the following questions without thinking. The longer your answers, the more marks you will get. If you give very short answers, or answers without a verb, you will lose marks.

🔊 **¿Vives en una casa o un piso?**
🔊 Vivo en una casa/un piso.
🔊 **¿Cómo es tu casa?**
🔊 Mi casa es pequeña y confortable.
🔊 **¿A qué distancia se encuentra tu casa del colegio?**
🔊 Se encuentra a cinco kilómetros de mi colegio.
🔊 **¿Cuántas habitaciones hay en tu casa?**
🔊 Hay … habitaciones.

You could name the rooms and get more marks.

Add a few more details!

¿Qué ves por la ventana de tu dormitorio?

Veo las casas de mis vecinos.

¿Qué hay en tu jardín?

Hay flores y árboles.

¿Qué hay en tu dormitorio?

Hay una cama, una mesa y una silla.

Conversation: Grades C–A*

AQA	✓
OCR	✓
EDEXCEL	✗
WJEC	✓
CCEA	✓

Remember to…

● use long sentences
● use past, present and future tenses
● give opinions
● justify your opinions.

Describe tu casa.

Mi casa es muy bonita. Hay tres dormitorios, una cocina, un comedor, una sala de estar y un cuarto de baño.

Describe tu dormitorio.

Mi dormitorio es muy confortable. Hay una cama, una silla, una mesa, un estéreo, un televisor y muchos libros. Es mi habitación favorita.

¿Qué haces en tu dormitorio?[1]

Hago muchas cosas. Hago mis deberes, leo, escucho música, veo la televisión y duermo, por supuesto.[2]

¿Qué hiciste anoche en tu dormitorio?

Hice mis deberes, leí, escuché música, vi la tele y por supuesto dormí.[3]

¿Qué harás esta tarde en tu dormitorio?[4]

Haré mis deberes, escucharé música, leeré, veré la tele y por supuesto dormiré.

Describe tu cocina.

Mi cocina es muy moderna. Hay una nevera, un lavaplatos, una lavadora y una mesa con cuatro sillas. Desde la cocina se ve el jardín.

Describe tu sala de estar.

Mi sala de estar es muy confortable. Hay un sofá, dos sillones, una alfombra roja, un televisor, un estéreo y cortinas muy bonitas.

¿Tienes un jardín?

Sí, tenemos un jardín detrás de la casa. Es muy bonito. Hay un césped, árboles, plantas y flores. También hemos[5] plantado patatas, cebollas, guisantes y zanahorias. A mis padres les gusta ocuparse[6] del jardín.

1 A chance to use the present tense.

2 'Por supuesto' means 'of course'.

3 Remember, use at least five preterites; one or two should be irregular for maximum effect.

4 Now five future tenses (see pages 123–124).

5 A perfect tense! This gets you more marks.

6 This 'gustar' construction is difficult and will get you extra marks.

Town, neighbourhood and region

AQA	✓
OCR	✓
EDEXCEL	✓
WJEC	✓
CCEA	✓

You may be asked to describe your town or region in the controlled assessment. Weather is often tested in the listening and reading exams. The following vocabulary will help you.

The environment (El entorno)

la luna

el árbol – tree
el arroyo – stream
el bosque – wood, forest
el camino – path
el/la campesino/a – peasant
el campo – countryside, field
la carretera – road
el cielo – sky

la ciudad – city, (large) town
la colina – hill
la estrella – star
la granja – farm
la isla – island
el lago – lake
la luna – moon
el mar – sea
la montaña – mountain

el mundo – world
el país – country
el paisaje – landscape
el pueblo – (small) town, village
la región – region
el río – river
el sendero – path
la tierra – earth, land

Animals (Los animales)

el animal – animal
el burro – donkey
el caballo – horse
el cerdo – pig

la gallina – hen
el insecto – insect
la oveja – sheep
el pájaro – bird

la rata – rat
el ratón – mouse
el toro – bull
la vaca – cow

Directions (Las direcciones)

la brújula

allá, allí – there
por allí – over there
la brújula – compass
cerca de – near
debajo de – beneath
a la derecha – to the right
todo derecho, todo recto – straight on

encima de – above
enfrente de – opposite
el este – east
a la izquierda – to the left
lejos de – far from
el noreste – north-east
el noroeste – north-west
el norte – north

el oeste – west
¿Para ir a...? – How do I get to...?
rodeado/a de – surrounded by
el sudeste – south-east
el sur – south
el suroeste – south-west

The weather (El tiempo)

el buen tiempo – good weather
el calor – heat
el chubasco – shower
el cielo – sky
el clima – climate
la escarcha – frost
la estación del año – season

el grado – degree
el hielo – ice
la lluvia – rain
el mal tiempo – bad weather
la neblina – mist
la niebla – fog
la nieve – snow
la nube – cloud
la nubosidad – cloudiness

el pronóstico del tiempo – weather forecast
el relámpago – lightning
el sol – sun
la temperatura – temperature
la tempestad – storm
la tormenta – storm
el trueno – thunder
el viento – wind

hace frío

Weather verbs

hace buen tiempo – the weather is nice
hace calor – the weather is hot
hace fresco – the weather is cool
hace frío – the weather is cold

hace mal tiempo – the weather is bad
hace sol – the weather is sunny
hace viento – the weather is windy

In the street (En la calle)

el cruce

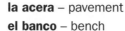

la acera – pavement
el banco – bench
el buzón – post box
la cabina telefónica – phone box
la calle – street
el carnet de identidad – ID card
el cartel – poster
la circulación – traffic
la cola – queue
el cruce – crossroads, junction

el embotellamiento – traffic jam
la esquina – corner
el estanco – tobacconist's
el letrero – sign
el monumento – monument
la parada de autobuses – bus stop
el paso a nivel – level crossing

el paso de peatones – pedestrian crossing
el peatón – pedestrian
prohibido el paso – no entry
el quiosco – kiosk
el ruido – noise
el semáforo – traffic light
sentido único – one-way
el tráfico – traffic

In town (En el centro)

la fuente

las afueras – outskirts
el alcalde – mayor
los alrededores – outskirts
el aparcamiento – car park
el apartamento – flat
la avenida – avenue
el ayuntamiento – town hall
el banco – bank
el bar – bar

el barrio – district, neighbourhood
la capital – capital
el centro – centre
la ciudad – city
el edificio – building
la estatua – statue
la fuente – fountain
el parque – park
el parque infantil – playground

el plano – town map
la plaza mayor – main square
la piscina – swimming pool
el piso – flat
la población – population
el pueblo – town, village
el puente – bridge
la torre – tower

Buildings (Los edificios)

la catedral

el albergue juvenil – youth hostel
la biblioteca – library
el bloque de pisos – block of flats
el castillo – castle
la catedral – cathedral
el centro comercial – shopping centre
el centro deportivo – sports centre
el cine – cinema
la comisaría – police station
correos (m, sing) – post office

la estación de autobuses – bus station
el hospital – hospital
la iglesia – church
el museo – museum
la oficina de objetos perdidos – lost property office
la oficina de turismo – tourist office
la plaza de toros – bullring
el polideportivo – sports centre
el teatro – theatre

Conversation: Grades G–D

AQA ✓
OCR ✓
EDEXCEL ✓
WJEC ✓
CCEA ✓

🔵 **¿Qué lugares de interés hay cerca de tu casa?**
⚪ Hay una iglesia interesante y un parque.
🔵 **¿A qué distancia se encuentra tu casa de Londres/del mar?**
⚪ Se encuentra a cien kilómetros de Londres/del mar.
🔵 **¿Cuántos habitantes tiene tu pueblo/ciudad?**
⚪ Hay ocho mil habitantes más o menos.
🔵 **¿Qué se puede hacer en tu pueblo/ciudad?**
⚪ Hay cines, discotecas y un club para jóvenes.

> The only verbs used here are 'hay' and 'se encuentra', which is why the conversation is grade G–D.

Conversation: Grades C–A*

AQA ✓
OCR ✓
EDEXCEL ✓
WJEC ✓
CCEA ✓

🔵 **Describe tu pueblo/ciudad/región. ¿Te gusta?**
⚪ A mí me gusta esta región. Porque aquí hay muchas cosas de interés. Hay un canal, un río, un parque bonito y muchas instalaciones deportivas y un cine. No lejos de aquí hay fábricas pero también hay campo bonito.
🔵 **¿Dónde en Gran Bretaña se encuentra tu región?**
⚪ Se encuentra en el norte/sur/este/oeste/centro de Inglaterra/Gales/ Escocia/Irlanda.
🔵 **¿Desde hace cuántos años vives aquí?**
⚪ Vivo aquí desde hace quince años, es decir toda mi vida.
🔵 **¿Cuáles son los edificios interesantes?**
⚪ Hay la biblioteca, el cine, el ayuntamiento, la vieja iglesia, la piscina y el hospital. También hay muchos edificios muy antiguos.
🔵 **¿Naciste en esta región?[1]**
⚪ Sí, nací a cinco kilómetros de aquí.
🔵 **¿Dónde vivirás en el futuro?[2]**
⚪ Viviré en esta región porque me gusta.
🔵 **¿Qué tiempo hace?**
⚪ Hace buen tiempo.
🔵 **¿Ayer qué tiempo hizo?**
⚪ Hizo mal tiempo.
🔵 **¿Qué tiempo hará mañana?**
⚪ Hará sol todo el día.

> 1 Your chance to use a preterite tense.
> 2 Your chance to use a future tense (see pages 123–124).

PROGRESS CHECK

Say or write the following in Spanish:
1 Bus stop
2 Police station
3 Wood
4 Horse
5 North
6 Wind
7 It is hot.
8 It was cold.
9 It is going to rain.
10 I would like to live in the country.

1. La parada de autobuses   2. La comisaría   3. El bosque   4. El caballo   5. El norte
6. El viento   7. Hace calor.   8. Hacía frío.   9. Va a llover.   10. Me gustaría vivir en el campo.

5.3 The environment

LEARNING SUMMARY	After studying this section, you should be able to:

After studying this section, you should be able to:

- name different endangered species
- describe and give views about dangers to the environment
- talk about how you help the environment

Environmental issues

AQA	✓
OCR	✓
EDEXCEL	✗
WJEC	✓
CCEA	✓

The following vocabulary and sentences will help you in the listening and reading exams, and in the controlled assessment.

Endangered species (La especie amenazada)

la ballena – whale
el delfín – dolphin
el elefante – elephant
la foca – seal
el guepardo – cheetah
el murciélago – bat

el/la oso/a – bear
los pájaros – birds
el/la panda – panda
los peces (m) – fish
el rinoceronte – rhino
el/la tigre(sa) – tiger

Dangers to the environment

Debemos proteger las especies amenazadas.
We should protect threatened species.
La ballena está en peligro de extinción.
The whale is in danger of extinction.
El mar contaminado mata a los peces.
The polluted sea is killing the fish.
El calentamiento global amenaza a los osos polares.
Global warming threatens polar bears.
No se debe matar a las ballenas.
We should not kill whales.

> **KEY POINT**
>
> **No se debe** and **no debemos** both mean 'we should not'.

The local environment

Mi ciudad es tranquila/ruidosa/industrial.
My city is quiet/noisy/industrial.
El aire está sucio/contaminado/limpio.
The air is dirty/polluted/clean.
Hay demasiadas fábricas y coches.
There are too many factories and cars.
La gente tira papeles al suelo.
People drop litter.

El aire y el río se contaminan.

The air and the river get polluted.

Necesitamos un centro de reciclaje.

We need a recycling facility.

Los gases del tubo de escape contaminan el aire.

Exhaust fumes pollute the air.

Los atascos en la hora de punta contaminan el aire.

The traffic jams at rush hour pollute the air.

No se usa el transporte público.

People do not use public transport.

Hay que mejorar el transporte público.

We must improve public transport.

> **KEY POINT**
>
> **Hay** means 'there is' or 'there are' but **hay que** means 'it is necessary to' or 'one must'.

Han creado zonas peatonales y carriles para bicicletas.

They have created pedestrian zones and cycle lanes.

No se permiten coches en el centro de la ciudad.

Cars are banned from the city centre.

Hay que pagar las bolsas de plástico.

You have to pay for plastic bags.

Debemos construir menos carreteras y aeropuertos nuevos.

We should build fewer new roads and airports.

What I do for the environment

Hago lo que puedo para proteger el entorno.

I do what I can to protect the environment.

Voy en bicicleta.

I cycle.

Voy a pie.

I walk.

Uso el transporte público.

I use public transport.

Recojo papeles en el parque.

I pick up litter in the park.

Apago las luces y cierro los grifos.

I switch off lights and turn off taps.

Animo a la gente a no usar el coche.

I encourage people not to use their car.

Reciclo cartón, papel, botellas, plástico, vídrio, latas y embalaje.

I recycle cardboard, paper, bottles, plastic, glass, tins and packaging.

Reutilizo bolsas de plástico.

I re-use plastic bags.

Adjectives

contaminado/a – polluted

limpio/a – clean

mundial – worldwide

renovable – renewable

ruidoso/a – noisy

tranquilo/a – calm, quiet

sucio/a – dirty

superpoblado/a – overpopulated

Issues (Las cuestiones)

la lluvia ácida

la basura – rubbish

el calentamiento del planeta – global warming

la capa de ozono – ozone layer

el carbón – coal

el consumo de energía – energy consumption

el cubo de la basura – dustbin

la deforestación – deforestation

el efecto invernadero – greenhouse effect

la energía nuclear – nuclear energy

la energía renovable – renewable energy

la energía solar – solar energy

la gasolina – petrol

el humo – smoke

la lluvia ácida – acid rain

el medio ambiente – environment

la paz – peace

los recursos naturales – natural resources

la Tierra – the Earth

los vertidos nucleares – nuclear waste

Verbs

aumentar – to increase

amenazar – to threaten

conservar – to conserve

crear – to create

dañar – to damage

desaparecer – to disappear

despilfarrar – to waste

destruir – to destroy

limpiar – to clean

malgastar – to waste

mejorar – to improve

producir – to produce

proteger – to protect

reducir – to reduce

salvar – to save

verter – to dump

5.4 Grammar

After studying this section, you should be able to understand:

- the imperfect tense
- direct object pronouns
- the personal **a**
- demonstrative adjectives
- the future tense
- possessive adjectives
- **ser** and **estar**

The imperfect tense

AQA	✓
OCR	✓
EDEXCEL	✓
WJEC	✓
CCEA	✓

KEY POINT

The imperfect tense is used for things that 'used to happen' or 'were happening', e.g. 'I used to play football', 'I was going to the cinema', etc. It is often used to describe situations in the past, e.g. 'it was raining', 'she was wearing a coat', etc.

To form the imperfect, add the **-aba** endings to the stems of **-ar** verbs and the **-ía** endings to the stems of **-er** and **-ir** verbs.

hablar	
hablaba	I was speaking; I used to speak
hablabas	you were speaking; you used to speak
hablaba	he/she was speaking; you were speaking; he/she/you used to speak
hablábamos	we were speaking; we used to speak
hablabais	you were speaking; you used to speak
hablaban	they/you were speaking; they/you used to speak

comer	
comía	I was eating; I used to eat
comías	you were eating; you used to eat
comía	he/she was eating; you were eating; he/she/you used to eat
comíamos	we were eating; we used to eat
comíais	you were eating; you used to eat
comían	they/you were eating; they/you used to eat

vivir	
vivía	I was living; I used to live
vivías	you were living; you used to live
vivía	he/she was living; you were living; he/she/you used to live
vivíamos	we were living; we used to live
vivíais	you were living; you used to live
vivían	they/you were living; they/you used to live

Irregular imperfects

There are only three irregular imperfects. They are shown in the table below.

ver

ir (to go)	ser (to be)	ver (to see)
iba	era	veía
ibas	eras	veías
iba	era	veía
íbamos	éramos	veíamos
ibais	erais	veíais
iban	eran	veían

PROGRESS CHECK

Say or write the following in Spanish:
1. I was wearing my new jersey.
2. It was raining.
3. I used to go to a different school.
4. He was my friend.

1. Llevaba mi jersey nuevo.
2. Llovía.
3. Iba a otro instituto.
4. Era mi amigo/a.

Direct object pronouns

AQA ✓
OCR ✓
EDEXCEL ✓
WJEC ✓
CCEA ✓

Study these sentences.

él **me** ve	he sees me	él **nos** ve	he sees us
él **te** ve	he sees you	él **os** ve	he sees you
él **le/lo** ve	he sees him/it/you	él **les/los** ve	he sees them/you
él **la** ve	he sees her/it/you	él **las** ve	he sees them/you

Pronouns normally come before the verb. When there are two parts to a verb (the auxiliary or modal and the main verb), the pronoun usually comes before the first part (the auxiliary or modal), e.g.:

Me ha visto.   He has seen me.

Pronouns are attached to the end of the verb...

- when it is an infinitive (i.e. it ends in **-ar**, **-er** or **-ir**), e.g.:

  Voy a hacerlo.   I am going to do it.

- when it is a present participle (i.e. it ends in **-ando** or **-iendo**), e.g.:

  Estoy haciéndolo.   I am doing it.

- when it is a positive command (imperative), e.g.:

  ¡Escúchame!   Listen to me!
  ¡No le escuches!   Don't listen to him!

KEY POINT

Note that when a pronoun is added to a present participle, you need to add an accent to maintain the stress. But this does not happen with negative commands.

The personal 'a'

AQA	✓
OCR	✓
EDEXCEL	✓
WJEC	✓
CCEA	✓

When the direct object of a sentence is a person, **a** is placed before the person, e.g.:

Visité a Juan.	I visited Juan.
Visité la catedral.	I visited the cathedral.

The preposition **a** is generally used with animals too, e.g.:

¿Has visto al perro?   Have you seen the dog?

> If you use a personal 'a' in your controlled speaking and/or writing assessment, you will impress the examiner, so why not learn a few examples?

PROGRESS CHECK

Say or write the following in Spanish:
1. I saw my friends.
2. I saw the famous places.

2. Vi los sitios famosos.
1. Vi a mis amigos.

Demonstrative adjectives

AQA	✓
OCR	✓
EDEXCEL	✓
WJEC	✓
CCEA	✓

KEY POINT

The demonstrative adjectives in English are 'this', 'that', 'these' and 'those'.

Look at these examples.

este chico	this boy	ese chico	that boy	aquel chico	that boy
esta chica	this girl	esa chica	that girl	aquella chica	that girl
estos chicos	these boys	esos chicos	those boys	aquellos chicos	those boys
estas chicas	these girls	esas chicas	those girls	aquellas chicas	those girls

Notice there are two ways of saying 'that' and 'those'. People or things that are referred to by **aquel**, etc., are further away than people or things referred to by **ese**, etc.

Me gusta ese libro pero no me gusta aquel libro.
I like that book, but I don't like that book (i.e. over there).

PROGRESS CHECK

Say or write the following in Spanish:
1. That book
2. This book
3. These books
4. Those books
5. That chair
6. This chair
7. These chairs
8. Those chairs

1. Ese/Aquel libro   2. Este libro   3. Estos libros   4. Esos/Aquellos libros   5. Esa/Aquella silla   6. Esta silla   7. Estas sillas   8. Esas/Aquellas sillas

The future tense

AQA ✓
OCR ✓
EDEXCEL ✓
WJEC ✓
CCEA ✓

Regular futures

To form the future tense in Spanish, you add the following endings to the infinitive:

-é, -ás, -á, -emos, -éis, -án

hablar		comer		vivir	
hablaré	I will speak	**comeré**	I will eat	**viviré**	I will live
hablarás	you will speak	**comerás**	you will eat	**vivirás**	you will live
hablará	he/she/you will speak	**comerá**	he/she/you will eat	**vivirá**	he/she/you will live
hablaremos	we will speak	**comeremos**	we will eat	**viviremos**	we will live
hablaréis	you will speak	**comeréis**	you will eat	**viviréis**	you will live
hablarán	they/you will speak	**comerán**	they/you will eat	**vivirán**	they/you will live

Irregular futures

Irregular futures all have the same endings.

querer

decir (to say)	hacer (to do/make)	poner (to put)
diré	**haré**	**pondré**
dirás	**harás**	**pondrás**
dirá	**hará**	**pondrá**
diremos	**haremos**	**pondremos**
diréis	**haréis**	**pondréis**
dirán	**harán**	**pondrán**
haber (to have)	poder (to be able)	querer (to want)
habré	**podré**	**querré**
habrás	**podrás**	**querrás**
habrá	**podrá**	**querrá**
habremos	**podremos**	**querremos**
habréis	**podréis**	**querréis**
habrán	**podrán**	**querrán**

saber (to know)	tener (to have)
sabré	tendré
sabrás	tendrás
sabrá	tendrá
sabremos	tendremos
sabréis	tendréis
sabrán	tendrán
salir (to go out)	venir (to come)
saldré	vendré
saldrás	vendrás
saldrá	vendrá
saldremos	vendremos
saldréis	vendréis
saldrán	vendrán

PROGRESS CHECK

Say or write the following in Spanish:
1. I will work
2. I will put
3. I will be
4. I will do

1. Trabajaré 2. Pondré
3. Seré/Estaré 4. Haré

Possessive adjectives

AQA ✓
OCR ✓
EDEXCEL ✓
WJEC ✓
CCEA ✓

KEY POINT

Possessive adjectives are used to describe possession. In English, they are 'my', 'your', 'his', 'her', 'its', 'our', 'their'.

Look at these examples.

1 Remember that, in the singular, 'tu'/'tus' is used for 'you' (familiar) and 'su'/ 'sus' for 'you' (polite).

2 Note that 'nuestro' and 'vuestro' are the only forms that change for masculine/feminine.

3 In the plural, 'vuestro/ a/os/as' is used for 'you' (familiar) and 'su'/'sus' for 'you' (polite).

mi libro	my book	mis libros	my books
tu[1] libro	your book	tus[1] libros	your books
su libro	his book	sus libros	his books
su libro	her book	sus libros	her books
su[1] libro	your book	sus[1] libros	your books

nuestro[2] hermano	our brother	nuestros[2] hermanos	our brothers
nuestra[2] hermana	our sister	nuestras[2] hermanas	our sisters
vuestro[3] hermano	your brother	vuestros[3] hermanos	your brothers
vuestra hermana	your sister	vuestras hermanas	your sisters
su libro	their book	sus libros	their books
su libro[3]	your book	sus libros[3]	your books

KEY POINT

In Spanish, the possessive adjectives agree with the object possessed (e.g. the book), not the person possessing them.

PROGRESS CHECK

Say or write the following in Spanish:
1. My dog
2. Your book (tú)
3. His car
4. Her car
5. Our house
6. Their friends

1. Mi perro 2. Tu libro 3. Su coche (de él) 4. Su coche (de ella) 5. Nuestra casa 6. Sus amigos (de ellos)

'Ser' and 'estar'

AQA	✓
OCR	✓
EDEXCEL	✓
WJEC	✓
CCEA	✓

Both **ser** and **estar** mean 'to be'. To work out which to use, the following formula is useful:

- In a 'who' situation, use **ser**, e.g.:

¿Quién es? Es nuestro profesor.	Who is he? He is our teacher.
Él es francés y ella es belga.	He is French and she is Belgian.

- In a 'what' situation, use **ser**, e.g.:

¿Qué es eso? Es una mesa.	What is that? It's a table.

- In a 'when' situation, use **ser**, e.g.:

¿Qué hora es? Son las dos.	What time is it? It is two o'clock.
¿Qué fecha es? Es el dos de mayo.	What's the date? It's the second of May.
Es verano.	It's summer.

- In a 'where' situation, use **estar**, e.g.:

¿Dónde está la estación? Está allí.	Where is the station? It's there.

- In a 'what like' situation, you must work out whether the description refers to a temporary characteristic or a permanent characteristic. If the characteristic is temporary, use **estar**; if permanent, use **ser**, e.g.:

El cielo está azul.	The sky is blue (but it may well change colour soon).
La puerta es azul.	The door is blue (although it may be repainted, the colour is a fairly permanent feature of the door).

PROGRESS CHECK

Say or write the following in Spanish:
1. I am a student.
2. Where is the station?
3. The house is green.

1. Soy alumno.
2. ¿Dónde está la estación?
3. La casa es verde.

Sample controlled assessment

Speaking

1 Track 28 You are going to have a conversation with your teacher about environmental problems. Your teacher will ask about…

- the kind of problems affecting the planet
- your attitude to flooding
- possible solutions.

Teacher: ¿Qué problemas hay con el medio ambiente?

Student: Maltratamos la Tierra. ¡Qué desastre! Cada año empeora la situación. Los habitantes de los países desarrollados usan demasiada energía. Cada uno consume el equivalente de 10 toneladas de carbón por año. El hombre es una especie en peligro de extinción. Quemamos las selvas que consumen el CO_2. En Brasil, hemos quemado millares de kilómetros cuadrados en un año. Contaminamos el aire, envenenamos los ríos y los mares, tratamos el planeta como un cubo de basura, modificamos las plantas y los animales, enterramos residuos nucleares y destrozamos nuestros recursos naturales. La capa de ozono desaparece por los gases de los tubos de escape. Esto produce el efecto invernadero y el calentamiento global. Es un círculo vicioso. Producimos gases tóxicos que suben en la atmósfera. El calor del sol sube también pero los gases lo bloquean. La Tierra se vuelve cada vez más caliente. Los mares suben y muchas especies están en peligro de extinción. Consumimos demasiada energía y por eso el planeta sufre.

Teacher: Y ¿las inundaciones?

Student: La nieve se derrite, los ríos se desbordan, los campos están inundados, las calles están sumergidas. La gente tiene que abandonar su hogar, las casas son destrozadas, el paisaje está arruinado y hay millares de muertos. Pronto no nos quedarán combustibles fósiles.

Teacher: Y ¿la solución?

Student: El gobierno cierra los ojos. Tenemos que cambiar nuestras malas costumbres, hay que hacer un plan de acción. No nos queda mucho tiempo. Hay que plantar árboles para reemplazar las selvas quemadas. Tenemos que usar transporte público para reducir la contaminación. Hay que ducharse en vez de bañarse para proteger los recursos de la Tierra y para reducir nuestro consumo de agua. Hay que reciclar todo. Debemos instalar paneles solares y doble vidrio y debemos aislar la casa. Hay que ir en bicicleta para reducir las emisiones de CO_2 y para reducir el consumo de gasolina. El coche representa la libertad pero también la polución. Sin coches, consumiríamos menos gasolina y tomando el bus o el tren, habría menos polución en el aire, el aire sería más limpio, haríamos más ejercicio, nos sentiríamos mejor y menos estresados.

Turn to page 156 for a translation of this passage.

Examiner's comments

This conversation is characterised by its impressive vocabulary:

'Empeorar' – to worsen

'Quemar' – to burn

'Envenenar' – to poison

'Enterrar' – to bury

'La capa' – layer

'El invernadero' – greenhouse

'Derretirse' – to melt

'El hogar' – home

'El combustible' – fuel

'Reemplazar' – to replace

'En vez de' – instead of

'Aislar' – to insulate

Sample controlled assessment

Writing

1 Write about how you help the environment. You could include…

- why we need to protect the environment
- what you do to help the environment during your daily routine
- what you do to save energy
- your attitude to car travel
- your attitude to recycling
- action you have taken to try to influence other people.

Hago lo que puedo para proteger[31] el medio ambiente. A pesar de[19] nuestros esfuerzos, nuestro planeta está a punto de morir.[21] ¡Qué desastre![9]

Voy en bicicleta o voy a pie pero no voy nunca[24] en coche. Decidí[4] hace mucho tiempo usar el transporte público. No tiro papeles al suelo. Hasta recojo[16] papeles en el parque. No malgasto nunca energía. Antes de salir[6] apago las luces y cierro los grifos. Mis padres han instalado paneles solares y ventanas dobles y nuestra casa está verdaderamente[18] bien aislada. Después de tomar[8] un baño o una ducha, riego el jardín con el agua que he usado.

Al hablar[7] con gente, les animo a dejar sus coches en casa. El coche representa la libertad pero también la polución. Sin el coche, el consumo de gasolina sería[14] menor. Debemos usar el bus y el tren y contaminaríamos menos la atmósfera, respiraríamos aire puro, haríamos más ejercicio, estaríamos menos estresados y nos sentiríamos mejor.[3]

En casa digo a todos que tenemos que reciclar. Reciclo cartón, papel, botellas, plástico y embalaje. Reutilizo las bolsas de plástico. Hacemos abono con los restos orgánicos. Uso pilas recargables para proteger el medio ambiente. Cuando compro papel por ejemplo, intento comprar papel hecho de materiales reciclados. Doy la ropa que ya no uso[24] a organizaciones benéficas. Antes de comprar[6] algo, me pregunto si lo necesito de verdad.

He escrito una carta al primer ministro. Le he dicho que debemos reducir el embalaje de cada producto, crear más centros de reciclaje, hacer carriles para bicicletas por todas partes en las ciudades, plantar árboles en las calles y mejorar el transporte público. Además le he dicho que prohíba los coches en el centro de la ciudad y las bolsas de plástico gratuitas. Debemos construir menos carreteras y aeropuertos nuevos.[15]

Turn to page 156 for a translation of this passage.

Examiner's comments

This excellent example is about the right length for an A* and it uses a number of the '32 points for improving your grade' from pages 8–9:

3 A justified point of view

4 A 'decidí' structure

6 Two examples of 'antes de…'

7 'Al' + the infinitive

8 'Después de' + the infinitive

9 An exclamation

14 An example of the conditional

15 One example of an adjective

16 An impressive structure

18 'Verdaderamente' has been used in place of 'muy'

19 'A pesar de'

21 'Estar a punto de'

24 Negatives have been used

31 'Para' + the infinitive

Exam practice questions

Listening

1 *Track 29* A Spaniard is talking about Valencia. Answer these questions about the city.

(a) Where in Spain is Valencia?

....

(b) Why is it an important city?

....

(c) Why do many English people live there?

....

(d) In what month are the famous festivals?

.... **(4)**

2 *Track 30* You want to go to the beach on Monday, Tuesday or Wednesday. Listen to the weather forecast and tick the appropriate box.

A Monday ☐

B Tuesday ☐

C Wednesday ☐ **(1)**

Reading

1 Match each sign with the correct sentence. Write the correct letter in the answer spaces.

A PESCADERIA GLORIA

C *i* OFICINA DE TURISMO

B BAR CAFETERIA

D FARMACIA

Sentence	Sign
(a) I want a drink.	....
(b) I want to buy fish.	....
(c) I want to buy aspirins.	....
(d) I want information.	.... **(4)**

Exam practice questions

2   **Winter**, **spring**, **summer** or **autumn**? Write the correct season in the answer spaces.

(a)   Durante la Semana Santa visitamos la granja de mi tío. ....

(b)   Mi cumpleaños es el diez de octubre. ....

(c)   Tenemos dos semanas de vacaciones en Navidades. ....

(d)   Practiqué el esquí en enero. ....

(e)   Hace mucho calor en el sur de España en agosto. ....

(f)   Me gusta tomar el sol en la playa en julio. .... **(6)**

3   Read the e-mail below and then tick the correct boxes to answer the questions that follow.

> Hola Conchi,
>
> Estoy en Valencia y voy a pasar quince días en Madrid con mi marido, José. Estaremos en un hotel de cinco estrellas. José es de Madrid y quiere llevarme a todos los restaurantes típicos y también quiere ver un partido de fútbol. La primera idea es excelente pero la segunda no me gusta. ¿El tiempo en Madrid? Es como un horno. Cuarenta grados todos los días. Menos mal que tenemos aire acondicionado.
>
> Saludos, Ana

(a)   Ana will be in Madrid for…

     A   a day   ☐   **B**   a week   ☐   **C**   a fortnight   ☐

(b)   The hotel will be…

     A   cheap   ☐   **B**   luxurious   ☐   **C**   mid-range   ☐

(c)   Ana…

     A   likes good food and dislikes football   ☐

     B   likes good food and football   ☐

     C   dislikes good food and football   ☐

(d)   The weather in Madrid is…

     A   cool   ☐   **B**   mild   ☐   **C**   hot   ☐   **(4)**

Education and work

The following topics are covered in this chapter:

- School and college
- Pressures and problems at school
- Jobs
- Grammar

6.1 School and college

LEARNING SUMMARY	After studying this section, you should be able to:
	• describe your school and school routine
	• understand information about a school in a Spanish-speaking country
	• say what you like and dislike about school, giving reasons

School and college

AQA	✓
OCR	✓
EDEXCEL	✓
WJEC	✓
CCEA	✓

Your teacher could ask you to describe your school in the controlled speaking assessment. You should prepare for all the obvious questions: questions about your subjects, the school building itself, the teachers and your plans for after school. You should realise that you may be tested on your tenses by questions about what you did yesterday at school and what you will do tomorrow. You may also be asked an opinion about your school. The following vocabulary will also help you in the listening and reading exams.

School (El instituto)

el examen

la **asignatura** – subject
la **atención** – attention
el **bachillerato** – A-level
la **clase** – class
el **colegio** – school
la **contestación** – answer
el **curso** – course
los **deberes** – homework
el **dibujo** – drawing
el **diccionario** – dictionary
el **ejemplo** – example
el **ejercicio** – exercise
el **error** – mistake
los **estudios** – studies
el **examen** – exam

la **frase** – sentence
la **gramática** – grammar
hacer preguntas – to ask questions
el **intercambio** – school exchange
el/la **interno/a** – boarder
la **lección** – lesson
la **letra** – letter (of the alphabet)
la **nota** – mark
el **número** – number
la **página** – page
la **palabra** – word
el **papel** – paper

el **permiso** – permission
la **pizarra** – blackboard
la **pregunta** – question
el **progreso** – progress
la **prueba** – test
el **pupitre** – desk
el **recreo** – break
la **respuesta** – answer
la **tarea** – homework
el **timbre** – bell
el **trimestre** – term
el **uniforme** – uniform
el **vocabulario** – vocabulary

	Lunes	Martes	Miércoles	Jueves	Viernes
09:00 – 10:10	geografía	inglés	ciencias	historia	francés
10:10 – 10:40	Recreo				
10:40 – 11:50	informática	español	física	tecnología	inglés
11:50 – 13:00	dibujo	tecnología	francés	informática	dibujo
13:00 – 15:00	Comida				
15:00 – 16:10	español	educación física	español	inglés	ciencias
16:10 – 16:20	Recreo				
16:20 – 17:30	ciencias	historia	informática	historia	español

Subjects (Las asignaturas)

el alemán – German
el arte – art
la biología – biology
el castellano – Spanish (language)
las ciencias – sciences
la economía – economics
la educación física – PE
el español – Spanish

la física – physics
el francés – French
la geografía – geography
la gimnasia – PE
la historia – history
los idiomas – languages
la informática – IT
el inglés – English
la literatura – literature

las matemáticas – maths
la música – music
la química – chemistry
el teatro – drama
la tecnología – technology
los trabajos manuales – CDT

Adjectives

aburrido/a – bored, boring
antiguo/a – old, former
ausente – absent
fácil – easy
festivo/a – holiday

incorrecto/a – incorrect
injusto/a – unfair
mixto/a – mixed
moderno/a – modern
particular – private, particular

pobre – poor
posible – possible
presente – present
probable – probable
severo/a – severe

el gimnasio

el laboratorio

la clase

Places (Los lugares)

el aula (f) – classroom
la cantina – canteen, dining area
la clase – classroom
el colegio mixto – mixed school
el colegio técnico – technical school
la escuela – primary school
el gimnasio – gym

el instituto – school
el laboratorio – laboratory
el pasillo – corridor
el patio de recreo – playground
la sala de música – music room
la sala de profesores – staff room

Equipment (El equipo)

el bolígrafo – pen	**el lápiz** – pencil
la calculadora – calculator	**el libro** – book
el cuaderno – exercise book	**el libro de texto** – textbook
la fotocopiadora – photocopier	**el ordenador** – computer
la goma – rubber	**la regla** – ruler
la hoja de papel – sheet of paper	**el sacapuntas** – pencil sharpener

People (La gente)

el/la alumno/a – pupil	**el/la estudiante** – student
el/la director(a) – headteacher	**el/la profesor(a)** – teacher

el director   el profesor, la profesora

levantar la mano

Verbs

aburrirse – to get bored	**fracasar** – to fail
acabar de – to have just	**inquietarse** – to worry
aprender – to learn	**interesarse por/en** – to get interested in
aprobar – to pass (an exam)	**levantar la mano** – to raise one's hand
arreglar – to sort out	**necesitar** – to need
comenzar – to begin	**ofrecer** – to offer
comprender – to understand	**olvidarse de** – to forget
copiar – to copy	**organizar** – to organise
corregir – to correct	**pasar lista** – to call the register
deber – to have to	**permitir** – to allow
dejar el colegio – to leave school	**preguntar** – to ask
deletrear – to spell	**preocuparse** – to worry
dibujar – to draw	**preparar** – to prepare
empezar – to begin	**querer decir** – to mean
enseñar – to teach	**repasar** – to revise
entender – to understand	**repetir** – to repeat
escoger – to choose	**responder** – to answer
escuchar – to listen	**sacar buenas notas** – to get good marks
estar aburrido/a – to be bored	**sacar malas notas** – to get bad marks
estar interesado/a en – to be interested in	**significar** – to mean
	suspender – to fail (an exam)
estudiar – to study	**terminar** – to finish
explicar – to explain	**traducir** – to translate

PROGRESS CHECK

Say or write the following in Spanish:
1 Chemistry
2 Pencil
3 To get bad marks
4 Easy
5 My school is modern and the teachers are nice.
6 I like history, but I prefer Spanish.

1. La química
2. El lápiz
3. Sacar malas notas
4. Fácil
5. Mi instituto es moderno y los profesores son simpáticos.
6. Me gusta la historia pero prefiero el español.

Conversation: Grades G–D

AQA ✓
OCR ✓
EDEXCEL ✓
WJEC ✓
CCEA ✓

Make sure you can answer the following questions without thinking. Get someone to ask you the questions so you can practise answering them without using the book.

¿Qué asignatura prefieres?
Prefiero el español.

¿Por qué?
Me gusta el/la profesor(a).

¿Cuál es la asignatura que te gusta menos?
La asignatura que me gusta menos es el francés.

¿Qué deportes practicas en el colegio?
Juego al fútbol/al tenis/al hockey.

¿Cómo vienes al colegio por la mañana?
Vengo a pie/en coche/en autocar.

¿Cómo viniste al colegio esta mañana?
Vine a pie/en coche/en autocar.

¿A qué hora llegas?
Llego a las nueve menos cuarto.

¿A qué hora empiezan las clases?
Empiezan a las nueve y veinte.

¿Cuántas clases tienes cada día?
Tengo cinco clases cada día.

¿Cuánto tiempo dura cada clase?
Cada clase dura una hora.

¿A qué hora es el recreo?
El recreo es a las once y veinte.

¿Cuánto tiempo dura el recreo?
El recreo dura veinte minutos.

¿Qué haces durante el recreo?
Hablo con mis amigos/as y como un bocadillo.

¿Cuántos alumnos hay en tu colegio?
Hay seiscientos alumnos en mi colegio.

¿Cuántos profesores hay en tu colegio?
Hay cuarenta profesores.

¿Qué haces durante la hora de comer?
Como mis bocadillos y juego al tenis.

The more you say, the more marks you will get.

Conversation: Grades C–A*

AQA ✓
OCR ✓
EDEXCEL ✓
WJEC ✓
CCEA ✓

Look for opportunities to…

- use different tenses
- give and justify opinions
- use extended sentences with impressive vocabulary.

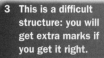

1 An opportunity to use a preterite.
2 The more you say, the more marks you will get.

¿Cómo viniste al colegio esta mañana?[1]

Vine a pie/en coche/en autocar.

¿Cómo te preparas para el colegio por la mañana?

Me despierto a las siete, me levanto a las siete y cuarto, me lavo, me visto y tomo el desayuno. Luego cojo los libros y me voy.[2]

Describe un día en tu colegio.

Llego a las nueve menos cuarto. Voy a mi clase y el profesor pasa lista. Luego voy a la primera clase. Hay otra clase y luego salgo al recreo.

¿Qué haces durante el recreo?

Charlo con mis amigos, como patatas fritas y bebo limonada.

Y ¿después?

Tenemos una clase más y luego es la hora de comer. A veces vuelvo a casa para comer, a veces como bocadillos y a veces como en la cantina. Luego hay dos clases más y vuelvo a casa y hago mis deberes.

Describe tu colegio.

Una parte del colegio es muy vieja y la otra parte es moderna. Hay campos de fútbol, pistas de tenis, laboratorios y una biblioteca. No tenemos piscina pero hay una muy cerca.

Háblame de tus asignaturas y tus clases.

Estudio ocho asignaturas, el inglés, las matemáticas, el español, la física, la química, la biología, la tecnología y el francés. Hay novecientos alumnos y sesenta profesores más o menos. Tenemos cinco clases diarias y cada clase dura una hora.

3 This is a difficult structure: you will get extra marks if you get it right.
4 An opportunity to use more preterites.
5 An opportunity to use future tenses.
6 An opportunity to give opinions and justify them.

¿Desde hace cuánto tiempo estudias el español?

Estudio el español desde hace[3] tres años.

¿Qué hiciste en tu instituto ayer?[4]

Llegué a las nueve, fui a mis clases, charlé con mis amigos, jugué al tenis y volví a casa.

¿Qué harás en tu instituto mañana?[5]

Iré a mis clases, hablaré con mis amigos, jugaré al baloncesto, comeré mis bocadillos y volveré a casa.

¿Te gusta tu instituto?[6]

Odio mi instituto porque los profesores nos dan demasiados deberes, son muy estrictos, no nos tratan como adultos y me marcharé lo antes posible.

6.2 Pressures and problems at school

<table>
<tr><td>**LEARNING SUMMARY**</td><td>**After studying this section, you should be able to:**

● describe the pressures and problems of school life
● explain what you must do and should not do at school</td></tr>
</table>

Pressures and problems at school

AQA ✓ OCR ✓ EDEXCEL ✓ WJEC ✓ CCEA ✓	The following words and phrases are useful when speaking or writing about the pressures and problems of school life. They will also help you in the listening and reading exams.

Pressures (Las presiones)

el boletín – school report	**los exámenes** – exams
el estrés – stress	**extraescolar** – extra-curricular
estresado/a – stressed	**las notas** – marks
estresante – stressful	

What is not allowed in school

llevar maquillaje

Está prohibido... Se prohibe... No podemos... No debemos... No se debe...	We are not allowed to...
escoger lo que llevamos	choose what we wear
llevar maquillaje o joyas	put on make-up or wear jewellery
hablar cuando habla el profesor	speak when the teacher is speaking
dar nuestras opiniones	give our opinions
ser insolente	be cheeky
fumar, comer, beber en clase	smoke, eat, drink in class
llegar tarde	arrive late
salir del instituto	leave the school
masticar chicle	chew gum

What we have to do in school

Tenemos que... Debemos... Hay que...	We have to...
trabajar duro	work hard
escuchar y respetar a los profesores	listen to and respect our teachers
llevar un uniforme feo	wear an ugly uniform
escuchar con atención todo el tiempo	pay attention all the time

Sources of stress

Estoy harto/a de mi instituto.

I am fed up with school.

No soy más que un nombre en una lista.

I am only a name on a list.

> **KEY POINT**
>
> **No ... más que** means 'only'.

Las reglas no son razonables.

The rules are unfair.

Un día en el colegio es estresante.

The school day is stressful.

Tengo un profe de lengua que no tiene autoridad y no sabe preparar sus clases.

I have a language teacher who has no authority and cannot prepare his/her lessons.

El uniforme es espantoso. Aunque sea bueno para la disciplina, es feo y poco elegante. Todo el mundo se parece.

The uniform is awful. Although it is good for discipline, it is ugly and not very elegant. Everybody looks the same.

'Sea' here is a subjunctive. Extra marks!

Hay violencia y graffiti.

There is violence and graffiti.

Me suspenden en todo, no progreso y todas mis notas son catastróficas.

I fail everything, I am not making progress and all my marks are catastrophic.

> **KEY POINT**
>
> **Suspender** means 'to fail'. **Me suspenden** literally means 'they suspend me'.

Tengo que sacar buenas notas todo el tiempo.

I have to get good marks all the time.

Los profes no nos escuchan y no nos comprenden.

The teachers do not listen to us or understand us.

Los profesores nos dan demasiados deberes.

The teachers give us too much homework.

Para hacer bachillerato, necesito buenas notas.

To do A-levels, I need good marks.

> **KEY POINT**
>
> **Bachillerato** is a two-year course taken by 17 and 18-year-olds in Spain.

Odio todas mis asignaturas y a todos mis profes.

I hate all my subjects and all my teachers.

No hay actividades extraescolares.

There are no extra-curricular activities.

No entiendo nada en química.

I understand nothing in chemistry.

El profesor no explica nada.

The teacher explains nothing.

Algunos alumnos hacen demasiado ruido y no oigo al profe.

Some pupils make too much noise and I cannot hear the teacher.

No tengo suficiente tiempo para hacer todo lo que exigen.

I do not have time to do everything they demand.

Nuestros padres ejercen demasiada presión sobre nosotros.

Our parents put too much pressure on us.

Trabajamos todo el tiempo y no tenemos tiempo para el ocio.

We work all the time and we do not have time for leisure activities.

Los profes no se interesan en mí.

The teachers are not interested in me.

Los campos de fútbol son demasiados pequeños.

The football pitches are too small.

No tenemos suficiente equipación.

We do not have enough equipment.

No me llevo bien con mis profesores.

I do not get on well with my teachers.

El ambiente en mi instituto es espantoso.

The atmosphere in my school is awful.

PROGRESS CHECK

Say or write the following in Spanish:

1. It is forbidden to smoke.
2. The school day is stressful.
3. The uniform is awful.
4. They give us too much homework.
5. I cannot hear the teacher.

5. No oigo al profe.
4. Nos dan demasiados deberes.
3. El uniforme es espantoso.
2. Un día en el colegio es estresante.
1. Está prohibido fumar.

6.3 Jobs

LEARNING SUMMARY	**After studying this section, you should be able to:** • talk about current and future jobs • outline your future plans • describe the advantages and disadvantages of different jobs

Current and future jobs

AQA	✓
OCR	✓
EDEXCEL	✓
WJEC	✓
CCEA	✓

You might have to talk about jobs and future plans in your controlled speaking and writing assessments. The future tense is going to be important. You should be ready to talk and write about your work experience. In the listening and reading exams, the words for all the different jobs are always coming up. Learn them!

la oficina

The world of work (El mundo del trabajo)

la ambición – ambition
el anuncio – advertisement
la carrera – career
el comercio – trade
la compañía – company
la computadora – computer
el despacho – (individual) office
el empleo – job
la empresa – firm
la entrevista – interview
la fábrica – factory
la finca – farm
el formulario – form
la fotocopia – photocopy

la solicitud de trabajo – job application form
la industria – industry
la máquina de escribir – typewriter
los negocios – business
la oferta – offer
la oficina – (large) office
el ordenador – computer
la profesión – profession
el proyecto – plan, project
el sindicato – trade union
el sueldo – pay
el trabajo – work
el turismo – tourism
la universidad – university

el arquitecto

Jobs (Los empleos)

el/la abogado/a – lawyer
el actor/la actriz – actor/actress
la ama de casa – housewife
el/la arquitecto/a – architect
el/la artista – artist
el/la autor(a) – author
el/la azafato/a – flight attendant
el/la bombero/a – firefighter
el/la cajero/a – cashier
el/la camarero/a – waiter/waitress
el/la camionero/a – lorry driver
el/la cantante – singer
el/la carnicero/a – butcher
el/la carpintero/a – carpenter
el/la cartero/a – postman
el/la chófer – driver
el/la cocinero/a – cook
el/la conductor(a) – driver
la criada – maid
el cura – priest
el/la dentista – dentist
el/la dependiente/a – shop assistant
el/la doctor(a) – doctor
el/la electricista – electrician
el/la enfermero/a – nurse
el/la escritor(a) – writer
el/la florista – florist
el/la fontanero/a – plumber
el/la fotógrafo/a – photographer
el/la frutero/a – fruit seller

el/la funcionario/a – civil servant
el/la garajista – garage attendant
el/la granjero/a – farmer
el/la guardia – traffic warden
el/la guía – guide
el/la hombre/mujer de negocios – businessman/woman
el/la ingeniero/a – engineer
el/la jardinero/a – gardener
el/la juez(a) – judge
el/la maestro/a – teacher (primary school)
el/la marinero/a – sailor
el/la mecánico/a – mechanic
el/la minero/a – miner
el/la obrero/a – worker
el/la panadero/a – baker
el/la peluquero/a – hairdresser
el/la periodista – journalist
el/la pescador(a) – fisherman
el/la piloto/a – pilot
el/la pintor(a) – painter
el/la policía – police officer
el/la profesor(a) – teacher, lecturer
el/la recepcionista – receptionist
el/la sastre/a – tailor
el/la secretario/a – secretary
el/la soldado/a – soldier
el/la taxista – taxi driver
el/la tendero/a – shopkeeper

la criada

la enfermera

Verbs

cuidar – to take care of

cultivar – to grow

diseñar – to design

emplear – to employ, to use

escribir – to write

estar en paro – to be unemployed

ganarse la vida – to earn your living

hacerse – to become

pagar – to pay

trabajar – to work

trabajar de canguro – to babysit

PROGRESS CHECK

Say or write the following in Spanish:
1. I want to be a doctor.
2. I do not want to work in an office.
3. I worked for a week in a hotel.
4. The work was interesting.

1. Quiero ser médico.
2. No quiero trabajar en una oficina.
3. Trabajé una semana en un hotel.
4. El trabajo era interesante.

Conversation: Grades G–D

AQA ✓
OCR ✓
EDEXCEL ✓
WJEC ✓
CCEA ✓

🎙 **¿Qué vas a hacer el año que viene?**

🎙 Voy a seguir con mis estudios. Voy a estudiar el inglés, el francés y por supuesto el español.

🎙 **Cuando termines tu bachillerato, ¿qué quieres hacer?**

🎙 Quiero ir a una universidad para estudiar idiomas.

🎙 **Y ¿después de la universidad?**

🎙 Quiero ser músico/a. Quiero hacer mucho dinero y ser muy famoso/a.

> This immediate future will get you extra marks.

Conversation: Grades C–A*

AQA ✓
OCR ✓
EDEXCEL ✓
WJEC ✓
CCEA ✓

🎙 **¿Qué tipo de trabajo has hecho?**

🎙 Durante mi semana de trabajo, trabajé en una oficina en el centro de la ciudad.

🎙 **Y ¿qué tenías que hacer?**

🎙 Tenía que hacer llamadas y escribir cartas.

🎙 **Y ¿te gustó el trabajo?**

🎙 Sí, me gustó pero no quiero hacer este tipo de trabajo en el futuro.

🎙 **¿En qué quieres trabajar?**

🎙 Quiero ir a la universidad para estudiar medicina, luego viajar por todo el mundo, luego trabajar en Londres. Seré médico.

> A good variety of tenses: preterite, imperfect and future.

Future plans/advantages and disadvantages of jobs

AQA	✓
OCR	✓
EDEXCEL	✓
WJEC	✓
CCEA	✓

The table below provides some good structures to help you express your views about different jobs.

Me gustaría No me gustaría Quiero No quiero Tengo ganas de No tengo ganas de	ser trabajar como	policía dentista profesor(a) secretario/a veterinario/a	porque	es no es está no está	agradable bien pagado maravilloso difícil duro aburrido fácil cansador interesante mal pagado monótono satisfactorio estresante variado
	trabajar	al aire libre dentro de un edificio			
		en	una oficina una tienda un banco una fábrica una escuela primaria un colegio un hospital negocios marketing el sector turístico informática	con	niños ancianos gente enfermos animales ordenadores

The following vocabulary and sentences will help you in the listening and reading exams, and in the controlled assessment.

los ordenadores

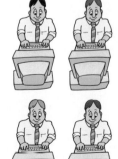

Describing work (Describiendo el trabajo)

aburrido/a – boring
agradable – pleasant
al aire libre – outside
bien pagado – well paid
cansador – tiring
comercio, negocio – business
como – as
con – with
dentro – inside
dentro de un edificio – indoors

difícil – difficult
duro/a – hard
estresante – stressful
fácil – easy
me gustaría – I would like
la informática – ICT
interesante – interesting
monótono/a – monotonous
los niños – children

los ordenadores – computers
mal pagado – badly paid
quiero... – I want...
satisfactorio/a – satisfying
ser – to be
tengo ganas de... – I want to, I feel like...
trabajar – to work
variado – varied

> **KEY POINT**
>
> If you find you are using **aburrido** (boring) too much, **monótono** is a good alternative.

What I want to do/what I want to be

Quiero ser periodista porque el trabajo es interesante y está bien pagado.
I want to become a journalist because the work is interesting and it is well paid.
Voy a hacerme médico porque me gusta ayudar a la gente.
I am going to become a doctor because I like helping other people.

> **KEY POINT**
>
> **Hacerse** means 'to become' when 'become' is followed by a noun. When 'become' is followed by an adjective, use **ponerse**.

He decidido que quiero trabajar al aire libre.
I have decided that I want to work outdoors.
Estoy seguro/a que no me gustaría hacerme profesor(a).
I am sure that I would not like to become a teacher.
Mi sueño es ser futbolista.
My dream is to be a footballer.
Voy a seguir con mis estudios.
I am going to carry on studying.
Iré a la universidad.
I will go to university.

hacer de canguro,
cuidar a/de los niños

Part-time work (Trabajo a tiempo parcial)

ayudar – to help
empezar/comenzar a – to begin to
ganar – to earn
hacer de canguro, cuidar a/de los niños – to babysit

pesado/a – heavy, tiring
recibir – to receive, to earn
repartir periódicos – to deliver papers
servir – to serve
terminar – to finish

> **KEY POINT**
>
> • **Empezar** and **comenzar** are radical-changing verbs. See pages 48–50 for more information.
> • **Canguro** really means 'a kangaroo'!

Part-time work

Tengo/busco un trabajo a tiempo parcial.
I have/am looking for a part-time job.
Tenía un trabajo a tiempo parcial.
I used to have a part-time job.
Servía a los clientes.
I used to serve the customers.

> **KEY POINT**
>
> Notice the use of the imperfect tense in the two sentences immediately above.

Necesito dinero.

I need money.

Los fines de semana trabajo en una tienda.

At weekends, I work in a shop.

Empiezo a las ocho y termino a las cinco.

I start at eight and finish at five.

Sirvo a los clientes.

I serve the customers.

Hago de canguro para mi hermana...gano quince libras.

I babysit for my sister...I get £15.

Reparto periódicos. No me gusta levantarme tan temprano. El trabajo está mal pagado. Llego al instituto cansado/a. Gano seis libras por hora. No me gustan los días de lluvia. No voy a hacerlo más. Quiero ganar dinero para poder comprarme maquillaje y CDs.

I deliver newspapers. I do not like getting up so early. The work is badly paid. I am tired when I get to school. I earn £6 an hour. I do not like the rainy days. I am not doing it anymore. I want to earn money to buy make-up and CDs.

Quiero ahorrar dinero para poder ir de vacaciones.

I want to save money to go on holiday.

Mis padres me dan un poco de dinero.

My parents give me some money.

Me dan veinte libras a la semana. Tengo que lavar el coche.

They give me £20 a week. I have to wash the car.

No es bastante.

It is not enough.

Work experience

En octubre, adquirí experiencia laboral durante una semana. No me pagaron.

In October, I did work experience for a week. I did not get paid.

Tenía que levantarme a una hora terrible.

I had to get up dreadfully early.

Trabajé en una oficina.

I worked in an office.

Empezaba a las ocho.

I started at eight.

Terminaba a las cinco.

I finished at five.

Iba en autobús.

I travelled by bus.

Ayudaba al jefe/a la jefa.

I helped the boss.

Llamaba a los clientes.

I phoned the customers.

Contestaba al teléfono.

I answered the phone.

Tenía un ordenador.

I had a computer.

Hacía el té.

I made the tea.

Fotocopiaba documentos.
I photocopied documents.
Atendía a los clientes.
I served the customers.
Mi experiencia laboral fue interesante/aburrida/ útil/inútil.
My work experience was interesting/boring/ useful/useless.
Mis colegas eras simpáticos/antipáticos.
The people were nice/nasty.

PROGRESS CHECK

Say or write the following in Spanish:
1. I want to work as a secretary.
2. I do not want to work outside.
3. My work experience was useful.
4. I want to be a journalist.
5. I will go to university.

1. Quiero trabajar como secretario/a.
2. No quiero trabajar al aire libre.
3. Mi experiencia laboral fue útil.
4. Quiero ser periodista.
5. Iré a la universidad.

6.4 Grammar

LEARNING SUMMARY

After studying this section, you should be able to understand:

- the conditional tense
- **conocer** and **saber**
- expressions with **tener**
- the pluperfect tense
- prepositions

The conditional tense

AQA ✓
OCR ✓
EDEXCEL ✓
WJEC ✓
CCEA ✓

KEY POINT

The conditional is recognised in English by the use of the word 'would' or sometimes 'should', e.g. I would go, I should like.

You should master the conditional if you want to get an A or A*. Its use will impress examiners, and you should try to include it in your controlled writing and speaking assessments.

Regular conditionals

In Spanish, you form the conditional by adding the endings used for the imperfect of **-er** and **-ir** verbs to the infinitive.

hablar		comer		vivir	
hablaría	I would speak	**comería**	I would eat	**viviría**	I would live
hablarías	you would speak	**comerías**	you would eat	**vivirías**	you would live
hablaría	he/she/ you would speak	**comería**	he/she/ you would eat	**viviría**	he/she/you would live
hablaríamos	we would speak	**comeríamos**	we would eat	**viviríamos**	we would live
hablaríais	you would speak	**comeríais**	you would eat	**viviríais**	you would live
hablarían	they/you would speak	**comerían**	they/you would eat	**vivirían**	they/you would live

Irregular conditionals

The irregular conditionals use the same stems as the irregular futures.

KEY POINT

Verbs that are irregular in the future are also irregular in the conditional.

hacer

decir (to say)	hacer (to do/make)	poner (to put)
diría	**haría**	**pondría**
dirías	**harías**	**pondrías**
diría	**haría**	**pondría**
diríamos	**haríamos**	**pondríamos**
diríais	**haríais**	**pondríais**
dirían	**harían**	**pondrían**
haber (to have)	poder (to be able)	querer (to want)
habría	**podría**	**querría**
habrías	**podrías**	**querrías**
habría	**podría**	**querría**
habríamos	**podríamos**	**querríamos**
habríais	**podríais**	**querríais**
habrían	**podrían**	**querrían**
saber (to know)	tener (to have)	
sabría	**tendría**	
sabrías	**tendrías**	
sabría	**tendría**	
sabríamos	**tendríamos**	
sabríais	**tendríais**	
sabrían	**tendrían**	
salir (to go out)	venir (to come)	
saldría	**vendría**	
saldrías	**vendrías**	
saldría	**vendría**	
saldríamos	**vendríamos**	
saldríais	**vendríais**	
saldrían	**vendrían**	

PROGRESS CHECK

PROGRESS CHECK

Say or write the following in Spanish:

1 He said he would come.

2 He said that they would go out.

1. Dijo que vendría.
2. Dijo que saldrían.

'Conocer' and 'saber'

AQA	✓
OCR	✓
EDEXCEL	✓
WJEC	✓
CCEA	✓

The verbs **conocer** and **saber** both mean 'to know'. **Conocer** is to know a person or a place, and **saber** is to know a fact or how to do something, e.g.:

Conozco Madrid muy bien.	I know Madrid very well.
¿No conoces a María?	Don't you know María?
Sé la hora pero no sé la fecha.	I know the time but not the date.
Ella sabe nadar y él sabe cocinar.	She can swim and he can cook.

PROGRESS CHECK

Say or write the following in Spanish:

1 I know Paul.

2 I know what he will do.

3 I can swim.

1. Conozco a Paul.
2. Sé lo que hará.
3. Sé nadar.

Expressions with 'tener'

AQA	✓
OCR	✓
EDEXCEL	✓
WJEC	✓
CCEA	✓

Note the following expressions that use **tener**. They will earn you lots of marks.

tengo quince años	I am fifteen
tengo calor	I am hot
tengo éxito	I am successful
tengo frío	I am cold
tengo hambre	I am hungry
tengo miedo	I am frightened
tengo prisa	I am in a hurry
tengo que irme	I have to go
tengo razón	I am right
tengo sed	I am thirsty
tengo suerte	I am lucky

PROGRESS CHECK

Say or write the following in Spanish:

1 I am hot.

2 I am cold.

3 I am hungry.

4 I am thirsty.

5 He is right.

6 She has to go.

7 We are lucky.

8 They are frightened.

1. Tengo calor.   2. Tengo frío.   3. Tengo hambre.   4. Tengo sed.   5. Tiene razón.
6. Tiene que irse.   7. Tenemos suerte.   8. Tienen miedo.

The pluperfect tense

AQA ✓
OCR ✓
EDEXCEL ✓
WJEC ✓
CCEA ✓

To form the pluperfect in Spanish, take the imperfect of **haber** and add the past participle.

hablar	
había hablado	I had spoken
habías hablado	you had spoken
había hablado	he/she/you had spoken
habíamos hablado	we had spoken
habíais hablado	you had spoken
habían hablado	they/you had spoken
comer	
había comido	I had eaten
habías comido	you had eaten
había comido	he/she/you had eaten
habíamos comido	we had eaten
habíais comido	you had eaten
habían comido	they/you had eaten
vivir	
había vivido	I had lived
habías vivido	you had lived
había vivido	he/she/you had lived
habíamos vivido	we had lived
habíais vivido	you had lived
habían vivido	they/you had lived

PROGRESS CHECK

Say or write the following in Spanish:

1 He said that he had finished.
2 He said that I had gone.

2. Dijo que me había ido.
1. Dijo que había terminado.

146

Pruebas

Prepositions

AQA	✓
OCR	✓
EDEXCEL	✓
WJEC	✓
CCEA	✓

Here are some useful, mark-winning prepositional phrases.

Salimos a pesar del tiempo.
We went out in spite of the weather.

Vive al lado de la iglesia.
He lives beside the church.

Corrió alrededor de la mesa.
He ran around the table.

La ciudad está cerca del mar.
The city is near the sea.

Jugó contra un equipo francés.
He played against a French team.

El banco está debajo del/bajo el árbol.
The bench is under the tree.

Se paró delante de la casa.
He stopped in front of the house.

Se escondió detrás de la puerta.
He hid behind the door.

Durante el viaje, durmió.
He slept during the journey.

Yo fui en vez de él.
I went instead of him.

Se encontraron enfrente del cine.
They met opposite the cinema.

Está entre los dos puntos.
It is between the two points.

Los distribuyó entre sus amigos.
He gave them out among his friends.

Viajó hacia el norte.
He travelled towards the north.

Vive lejos de aquí.
He lives far from here.

Todos fuimos salvo ella.
We all went except her.

Según el periódico, está muerto.
According to the paper, he is dead.

PROGRESS CHECK

Say or write the following in Spanish:

1. In front of the house
2. Behind the house
3. Between the houses
4. Opposite the house
5. According to the teacher

5. Según el profesor
4. Enfrente de la casa
3. Entre las casas
2. Detrás de la casa
1. Delante de la casa

Sample controlled assessment

Speaking

1 **Track 31** You are going to have a conversation with your teacher about your plans for the future. Your teacher will ask you to discuss…

- your plans for the future
- your reaction to work experience
- your plans for future study
- marriage.

Teacher: Y ¿tus planes para el futuro?

Student: Acabo de[20] realizar una semana de experiencia laboral y esto me[32] ha dado ideas para el futuro. Tenía que[1] levantarme a una hora horrible y trabajaba[13] en una oficina. Debía fotocopiar, contestar al teléfono, llamar a clientes y hacer el té. Al final de esta experiencia negativa,[16] decidí[4] que no quiero trabajar nunca[24] en una oficina.

Teacher: ¿Por qué?

Student: Porque[2] el trabajo era monótono. Muchas veces estuve a punto de[21] marcharme puesto que el trabajo era tan aburrido.[18] A pesar de que[19] mis colegas eran simpáticos, tenía ganas[1] de volver a casa. No era el tipo de trabajo que me habían prometido.[17] Mi jefe dijo que hiciese[25] el té para los demás. ¡Qué pérdida de tiempo![9] Fue una experiencia inolvidable.[15] Afortunadamente,[16] he aprendido lo que tengo ganas[1] de hacer y lo que no quiero hacer.

Teacher: Y ¿eso?

Student: Para empezar,[31] voy a seguir[12] con mis estudios porque[2] he visto que la gente sin títulos académicos tiene los peores puestos de trabajo.[23] Luego iré a la universidad para obtener[31] lo que necesito para conseguir un trabajo en una buena profesión. He decidido que no quiero trabajar al aire libre todo el tiempo y que no quiero trabajar en una oficina tampoco.[24] Estoy seguro/a que no me gustaría[14] ser un(a) profesor(a). Es verdad que mi sueño era hacerme estrella pero creo que quiero hacerme periodista porque[2] el trabajo es interesante, bien pagado y trabajaría[14] en una oficina y al aire libre.

Teacher: ¿Vas a casarte?

Student: No voy a casarme hasta la edad de 30 años luego tendré tres niños. Cuando termine mis estudios espero conocer a una buena compañera/un buen compañero. Estaré contento/a porque viviré la vida de la manera que yo he escogido. Viviré en una casa de lujo y seguiré trabajando mientras[30] mi compañero/a se queda en casa.

Teacher: ¿El matrimonio es importante?

Student: El matrimonio nos ayuda a tener una relación armoniosa con alguien. Es algo que une a la pareja. Voy a casarme porque es importante que los niños tengan estabilidad.

Turn to page 156 for a translation of this passage.

Examiner's comments

This student has boosted his/her grade by using plenty of the '32 points for improving your grade' from pages 8–9:

1 'Tener' structures

2 Several examples of 'porque'

4 A 'decidí' structure

9 An exclamation

12 An example of the future tense

13 An example of the imperfect

14 Conditionals have been included

15 One example of an adjective being used

16 Impressive vocabulary and structures, e.g. 'experiencia negativa', 'afortunadamente'

17 An example of the pluperfect

18 'Tan' has been used as an alternative to 'muy'

19 An 'a pesar de' structure

20 'Acabar de'

21 'Estar a punto de'

23 An example of the superlative

24 Negatives have been used

25 A subjunctive has been included

30 'Mientras' is a good connective

31 Examples of 'para' + the infinitive

32 Use of a pronoun

Sample controlled assessment

Writing

1 Write about the pressures of school life. You could include…

- your attitude to school
- things you like or dislike about school
- your attitude to your teachers
- the contribution of your parents
- a possible solution to your problems.

Estoy harto/a de mi instituto.[16] No me dan la calidad de enseñanza que me habían prometido.[17]

Soy estudiante aquí desde hace[26] cuatro años y para mí el día escolar es muy estresante y estoy a punto de[21] ponerme enfermo/a. Aquí no soy más que[24] un nombre en una lista. Las reglas no son razonables, está prohibido llevar maquillaje o joyas, dar opiniones, fumar, comer o beber en clase etc. Al levantarme,[7] tengo que ponerme un uniforme feo y espantoso. Aunque sea[25] bueno para la disciplina, es feo y poco elegante. Todo el mundo se parece. Es el peor instituto[23] de la región.

El ambiente en mi instituto es malo. Hay violencia y graffiti. Las actividades extraescolares no existen. Algunos alumnos hacen demasiado ruido y no oigo lo que dice el profe. Los campos de fútbol son demasiado pequeños y no hay suficientes equipaciones. ¡Qué desastre![9]

No me entiendo bien con mis profesores porque[2] no se interesan en mí.[3] No explican nada,[24] no nos escuchan y no nos comprenden. Nos dan demasiados deberes. Tengo un profesor de lengua que[30] no tiene autoridad y que no sabe preparar buenas clases. No entiendo nada[24] en sus clases.

A pesar de que[19] no tengo el tiempo de hacer lo que me[32] exigen, mis padres ejercen demasiada presión sobre mí sin darse[5] cuenta. Trabajo todo el día y no tengo tiempo para el ocio. Tengo que sacar buenas notas todo el tiempo. Me suspenden en todo, no progreso y mis notas son desastrosas. He decidido hacer bachillerato pero, por desgracia,[16] para hacerlo[31] necesito buenas notas.

Me gustaría ir[14] a otro instituto y acabo de[20] preguntar a mis padres si es posible.

Turn to page 156 for a translation of this passage.

Turn to page 156 for a translation of this passage.

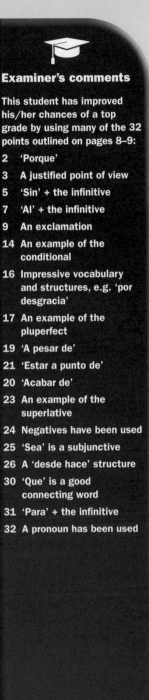

Examiner's comments

This student has improved his/her chances of a top grade by using many of the 32 points outlined on pages 8–9:

2 'Porque'

3 A justified point of view

5 'Sin' + the infinitive

7 'Al' + the infinitive

9 An exclamation

14 An example of the conditional

16 Impressive vocabulary and structures, e.g. 'por desgracia'

17 An example of the pluperfect

19 'A pesar de'

21 'Estar a punto de'

20 'Acabar de'

23 An example of the superlative

24 Negatives have been used

25 'Sea' is a subjunctive

26 A 'desde hace' structure

30 'Que' is a good connecting word

31 'Para' + the infinitive

32 A pronoun has been used

Exam practice questions

Listening

1 Track **32** Three students are talking about school. Tick the correct boxes.

		Pedro	Pilar	Enrique	
(a)	Who likes school?	☐	☐	☐	
(b)	Who does not go to lessons?	☐	☐	☐	
(c)	Who is longing for the end of term?	☐	☐	☐	
(d)	Who wants to be a teacher?	☐	☐	☐	
(e)	Who mentions a teacher that she/he likes?	☐	☐	☐	
(f)	Who mentions a teacher that she/he does not like?	☐	☐	☐	**(6)**

2 Track **33** Listen to José and Lolita and fill in the gaps.

José

Example: Subject he dislikes   Languages

(a) Favourite subject   ....

(b) Ambition   ....

(c) Favourite hobby   ....

Lolita

Example: Subject she dislikes   History

(d) Favourite subject   ....

(e) Ambition   ....

(f) Favourite hobby   ....   **(6)**

3 Track **34** Listen to this radio announcement. What are the two advantages of this job?

(a) ....

(b) ....   **(2)**

Exam practice questions

Reading

1 Read the article and fill in the spaces.

> **Carole Daly – entrevista con la reina de la cocina inglesa**
>
> Hasta hace poco, Carole vivía en Gales pero ahora tiene un apartamento de lujo en Londres, Inglaterra. Dice que la gente aprecia más su talento en la capital. Hoy en día vemos a Carole casi todos los días en la tele, dando consejos a los que quieren cocinar bien. Dice que gana el doble de lo que ganaba cuando era florista.
>
> – Cuando era estudiante, quería ser peluquera. Ahora esa idea no me interesa. Ahora mi ambición es ser la mejor cocinera del mundo.
>
> – Cometí un gran error. Me casé con Antonio. Luego me di cuenta que era un borracho y tuve que huir. Ahora mi marido es Jorge, un caballero elegante y simpático.
>
> – En Gales, tenía una casa enorme pero no me gustaba porque el jardín era una pesadilla. Menos mal que ahora tengo un piso.
>
> – Ahora tengo muy poco tiempo libre pero los fines de semana me gusta hacer footing en el parque. Antes mi pasión era el ajedrez pero ya no juego. Es mejor hacer ejercicio.

		In the past	Now
(a)	Country of residence	....	....
(b)	Occupation	....	....
(c)	Ambition	....	....
(d)	Name of husband	....	....
(e)	Type of residence	....	....
(f)	Favourite activity	....	.... **(12)**

2 Read the information below and answer the questions that follow.

> **Camping Internacional, Oviedo – necesita**
> • Guardas de seguridad/cocineros/camareros.
> • Experiencia mínima de dos años.
> • Pagamos bien. Temporada de verano.
> • Interesados deben enviar una foto reciente y una carta.
> • Se ruega abstenerse de llamar por teléfono.

(a) Name the three jobs that are being advertised.

   (i) .... (ii) .... (iii) .... **(3)**

(b) How much experience do you need? .... **(1)**

(c) What time of year is the work for? .... **(1)**

(d) What two things must you send?

   (i) .... (ii) .... **(2)**

(e) What must you not do? .... **(1)**

Exam practice answers

CHAPTER 1

Listening Task 1

(a) B; **(b)** F; **(c)** D; **(d)** A

Listening Task 2

(a) If they want a table for two.

(b) In the corner, far from the open window.

(c) The menu of the day

(d) Omelette

(e) Ham

(f) Salad

(g) Nothing

(h) Red wine

Listening Task 3

(a) (i) E **(ii)** A

(b) (i) F **(ii)** D

(c) (i) D **(ii)** B

(d) (i) A **(ii)** E

(e) (i) C **(ii)** C

Listening Task 4

B and D

Listening Task 5

(a) True; **(b)** False; **(c)** True; **(d)** True; **(e)** False;

(f) False; **(g)** True; **(h)** False; **(i)** False; **(j)** True;

(k) False

Listening Task 6

Section 1: The man: Apples, Grapes; The woman:
Ham, Milk

Section 2: The man: Bread, Sweets; The woman:
Flowers, Cereal

Reading Task 1

(a) C, D and E; **(b)** A; **(c)** D; **(d)** A; **(e)** D

Reading Task 2

(a) It is the most expensive.

(b) It helps you to maintain a balanced diet.

(c) Quality

(d) What you like

Reading Task 3

(a) A friend's house

(b) (i)–(iii) In any order: bad; pouring with rain; cold

(c) A lorry

(d) A broken arm

(e) A mobile phone

(f) The police station

(g) To thank him

Reading Task 4

(a) At any time

(b) Fish, meat and salad

(c) (i)–(iii) In any order: fry the onions slowly; use
free-range eggs; beat the eggs for only 30 seconds.

(d) They are made too quickly.

Reading Task 5

(a) Britain

(b) (i)–(ii) In any order: nature; sunny days

(c) Eat healthily

(d) (i)–(iv) In any order: chicken; tuna; salmon;
vegetables

(e) Fruit

(f) They do not spoil easily.

(g) A fridge

CHAPTER 2

Listening Task 1

(a) Carlos; **(b)** Rafael; **(c)** Luis; **(d)** Jaime;

(e) Enrique; **(f)** José

Listening Task 2

Juan: Art; Football; Bicycle

Elena: English; Basketball; Car

Sofía: German; Cycling; Bus

Enrique: Chemistry; Hockey; Walking

Listening Task 3

(a) C; **(b)** B; **(c)** A; **(d)** C; **(e)** A; **(f)** B

Reading Task 1

(a) For her e-mail

(b) María is not coming.

(c) That they are a waste of money

(d) They are better.

(e) To stay with her family

(f) To concerts and interesting places in London

(g) Peter

Reading Task 2

(a) (i) Give three days' notice **(ii)** Permission could
be withdrawn

(b) His friends

(c) Do something to deserve it.

(d) Arguing

(e) Weekends

(f) Let his parents know when he is coming home
after midnight.

(g) Not to be drunk

(h) Sleep all day

(i) She can go out twice a month.

(j) (i)–(iii) In any order: concerts; discos; parties

(k) Say what time she will be home

(l) She does

(m) Make choices

Reading Task 3

(a) (i)–(iii) In any order: he lost money; he fell ill; the flight was delayed.

(b) (i)–(iii) In any order: he lent him some money; he called a doctor; he let him stay another night.

(c) A present

(d) Andrew will go back to Spain.

Reading Task 4

(a) To eat ice cream

(b) Her boyfriend

(c) At a port

(d) A fisherman

(e) A mobile phone

(f) The fisherman returned it.

Reading Task 5

(a) Singer

(b) Fashion

(c) Her hair is longer.

(d) Sweden

(e) 22

(f) She gave a series of concerts.

(g) She was pregnant.

(h) She got married.

(i) (i) Painter **(ii)** Lawyer

(j) They are twins.

(k) He adores her.

(l) Her relatives

(m) To give presents to sick children.

(n) Cousin

(o) (i) He fell off his bike. **(ii)** He will never walk again.

CHAPTER 3

Listening Task 1

(a) A; **(b)** B; **(c)** C

Listening Task 2

(a) C; **(b)** B; **(c)** B, C and F

Listening Task 3

Carla: Likes a lot – Horror, Romantic; Likes a little – Westerns, Adventure

Fernando: Likes a lot – Westerns, Adventure; Does not like at all – Horror, Romantic

Listening Task 4

(a) Ice-skating

(b) All the clubs are run by professionals.

(c) Because the Peruvian Olympic team trained there.

(d) Basketball

(e) A gold medal

Listening Task 5

(a) False; **(b)** False; **(c)** True; **(d)** True; **(e)** True; **(f)** True; **(g)** True; **(h)** False; **(i)** True; **(j)** True

Listening Task 6

(a) B; **(b)** D; **(c)** A; **(d)** C

Listening Task 7

(a) legumbres; **(b)** baratos; **(c)** niños; **(d)** superior; **(e)** muebles; **(f)** gratuito

Reading Task 1

(a) A birthday; **(b)** C; **(c)** B; **(d)** B; **(e)** A; **(f)** A; **(g)** D

Reading Task 2

(a) Lead singer

(b) Ireland

(c) A painting

(d) When they were aged 14

(e) Ask questions

CHAPTER 4

Listening Task 1

(a) rucksack

(b) blue; car keys

(c) market; yesterday

Listening Task 2

(a) B; **(b)** A; **(c)** C; **(d)** A; **(e)** B; **(f)** C; **(g)** D; **(h)** B; **(i)** A; **(j)** A

Listening Task 3

(a) B; **(b)** C; **(c)** A; **(d)** C; **(e)** C; **(f)** A

Reading Task 1

(a) quincena; **(b)** París; **(c)** estupendo; **(d)** gente; **(e)** cocina; **(f)** ganas; **(g)** bien; **(h)** avería

Reading Task 2

(a) 34 24 40; **(b)** 31 25 00; **(c)** 77 40 40; **(d)** 32 20 00; **(e)** 81 21 20

Reading Task 3

(a) B; **(b)** A; **(c)** C; **(d)** D

Reading Task 4

(a) Bought a plane ticket

(b) Scotland

(c) At the beginning of the month

(d) (i) He doesn't know Scotland **(ii)** Mosquitoes

(e) West coast

(f) The islands

(g) Share a room

(h) Show him places

(i) Teach him to ride

(j) He is afraid of falling off.

(k) If they teach him some English.

(l) (i) Earn money **(ii)** Save

(m) (i) Delivers papers **(ii)** Gardening

Reading Task 5

(a) licores

(b) dormir

(c) vacío

(d) te quedes

(e) anterior

(f) lectura

(g) caras

(h) conversación

CHAPTER 5

Listening Task 1

(a) On the Mediterranean coast

(b) It has a port

(c) The climate

(d) February

Listening Task 2

B

Reading Task 1

(a) B; **(b)** A; **(c)** D; **(d)** C

Reading Task 2

(a) Spring; **(b)** Autumn; **(c)** Winter; **(d)** Winter;

(e) Summer; **(f)** Summer

Reading Task 3

(a) C; **(b)** B; **(c)** A; **(d)** C

CHAPTER 6

Listening Task 1

(a) Enrique; **(b)** Pedro; **(c)** Pedro; **(d)** Enrique;

(e) Pilar; **(f)** Enrique

Listening Task 2

(a) Biology

(b) To be a doctor

(c) Skating

(d) French

(e) To be a French teacher

(f) Reading

Listening Task 3

(a)–(b) In any order: you do not pay tax; lodging
is free

Reading Task 1

(a) Wales; England

(b) Florist; Cook

(c) To be a hairdresser; To be the best cook in
the world

(d) Antonio; Jorge

(e) House; Flat

(f) Chess; Jogging

Reading Task 2

(a) (i)–(iii) In any order: security guards; cooks;
waiters

(b) Two years

(c) Summer

(d) (i)–(ii) In any order: a recent photo; a letter

(e) Phone

Translated passages

CHAPTER 1
Speaking 1
Student: I have just returned from an unforgettable trip to Spain. My school has played a match annually for years against a Spanish school. The great adventure started three weeks ago. The whole team gathered very early in the morning in front of the school and we left for Spain by coach at six in the morning and after a long 24-hour journey we arrived at the school gate. Our host families were waiting for us.
Teacher: What did you do during the journey?
Student: During the journey, I read and I listened to music. Straight away, on our arrival, without wasting a moment we went to Pedro's house by car. His father was driving. His house was small but comfortable. There was a small charming garden with flowers and a lawn, but British gardens are the best in the world.
Teacher: Were you hungry?
Student: No. I did not want to eat. After a sleep, I went out to train. We did exercises and practised with the ball. Then we went back and spent the evening watching TV and chatting to my host family. Later, we went to a café for a drink and chatted to our Spanish friends. The atmosphere was marvellous.
Teacher: And the next day?
Student: The next day, my Spanish friend rejoined his friends. It was nice weather and the sun was shining. In spite of the heat, at 3pm, the match began. At the end of the first half we were winning 2-0 and I had scored one of the goals from a free kick. But just after half-time, what a disaster! I got injured.
Teacher: What happened?
Student: One of the Spanish players was angry because his team was losing. His tackle was very violent. He broke my leg. The pain was incredible. My team-mates were not happy either. My teacher called for an ambulance and it arrived ten minutes later. I stayed in hospital for three days and my friends came to see me every day. The hospital was pleasant and the nurses looked after me well.
Teacher: Did your friends bring you presents?
Student: Yes, they gave me fruit, chocolate and books. The whole Spanish team came to see me. The violent player said sorry. He gave me a gold watch as a present. His parents wrote to my parents to say sorry. I think that my visit to Spain was a disaster and I will never go back there. Let's hope not. It would not be a good idea.

Writing 1
Interview with Isabel Fretey – international star.
Everybody has heard of Isabel: the best female tennis player in Spain. By the age of 24 she had already won three competitions and this year she is going to try to win Wimbledon. A pretty Madrid girl, she is a true star. But her life has not always been easy.
– Isabel, tell us about your childhood.
– Life was hard. What a nightmare! My parents died when I was three and I went to live with my aunt in a rough area of Madrid. There were no facilities for playing tennis. To play, I had to take the tube and travel for an hour. But at last I found a good club. I had been a member for a year when I met Marcel who is now my trainer and my husband.
– And what do you do to stay fit?
– The important thing is to eat well. I never drink alcohol, I don't smoke and I exercise. And I play tennis with Marcel for four hours a day.
– And your first success?
– I won my first tournament in the USA. I was so happy. After winning, I celebrated the victory with a meal in a five-star restaurant.
– Apart from tennis, what do you like to do?
– I love reading. When I get home, I like to settle in an armchair and read a novel.
– And your family?
– I am an only child and my aunt is dead. But I have Marcel, my husband, and one day I hope to have children. But before having children, I want to win more tournaments. I must go to Wimbledon and I must win.
– And the problems of the world?
– For me, the main problem is the environment. People are not focussing on what is happening. We are in the process of destroying the planet.
– Isabel, good luck at Wimbledon.
– Thank you.

CHAPTER 2
Speaking 1
Teacher: Do you smoke?
Student: Absolutely not. It is so bad for your health. In the past I smoked regularly. I was addicted but after seeing a documentary on the dangers of smoking, I stopped. I have completely given up cigarettes and I don't smoke anymore. I haven't smoked for two years.
Teacher: Why?
Student: Tobacco contains substances that are dangerous for the heart, skin and especially the lungs so I don't feel like smoking any longer. The latest surveys are frightening. Now there are more girls than boys who smoke. Three girls out of ten smoke. In spite of the advice of her parents,

my sister smokes and it stinks. Her clothes smell bad and her teeth and fingers are yellow. It is so disgusting! But she says she is about to give up smoking.
Teacher: And the government?
Student: They have banned tobacco advertising, even the adverts on TV. Cigarette manufacturers try to attract young people. The multinationals even encourage us to smoke. In Africa they give out free cigarettes. What a scandal! What a nightmare! Unfortunately, cigarette manufacturers finance Formula 1 and youngsters can see the advertising on TV. We must tell the government to do more. They should make tobacco more expensive.
Teacher: Why do so many youngsters smoke?
Student: They smoke in order to look more grown up. There are people who smoke to be like their friends. They do it to look sophisticated. It is sociable. They say that cigarettes calm their nerves. They find it relaxing and it combats stress. If there is a problem, without delay, they take out their cigarettes.
Teacher: And passive smoking?
Student: When I see people smoking, I get angry. Passive smoking worries me. I am a victim of passive smoking and I have become asthmatic. Nobody has the right to make others suffer.
Teacher: Do you have any advice for children?
Student: Yes. Before starting to smoke, think. It is the worst thing that you can do. If you decide to smoke, you are going to regret it.

Writing 1
I am going to describe my future. I am going to be truly happy. It will be in a year, in two years or perhaps when I am thirty but it is happiness that I am looking for. I will be happy because I will lead my life in the way I have chosen. I want to get married.
I will not get married before thirty and I will have at least three children. Being a parent is part of my plans although I am frightened of the idea of having children. I want lots, lots of children, but before getting married I want to travel all over the world. After travelling, the important thing is love. I will live in a luxury house. When I finish my studies, I hope to find a good partner. When I meet him/her, I will know straight away if it is the person I need. When I finish university, I will marry a special person, perhaps a celebrity. I will be a house husband/wife. My partner will continue working while I will stay at home to look after the children.
For me, marriage is important for a good relationship. It is a link that unites a couple. I am going to get married because it is important for children to have stability. It is the most important thing in the world. I have just discussed this subject with my older sister. She says she does not understand why people get married. How awful!
She says it is simpler to co-habit without getting married. She is about to start living with her boyfriend. I will never co-habit despite the fact that my parents lived together before getting married. They had been living together for five years. My younger brother is neither for nor against marriage but he says that he does not want children unfortunately.

CHAPTER 3
Speaking 1
Teacher: What do you like doing?
Student: What I like most is sport. I like all sports but my favourite is tennis. I have been playing tennis for ten years, that is to say almost all my life. My parents encouraged me to play because they also play. I decided to become a member of a club when I was eight and I have just won my first competition.
Teacher: Do you do any other sports?
Student: I am about to join a horse-riding club. My parents gave me a horse last year. What a surprise! It is the most beautiful horse in the world. It is so intelligent. I began to ride when I was ten but I stopped because I had neither a horse nor money.
Teacher: What other activity do you like?
Student: I love films and the cinema. On Saturday evenings, although I don't have much money, I go to the cinema and my younger brother comes with me. Before going, we look for the best films on the Internet. After finding a good film, we go and see it in town. My brother likes horror films whereas I like drama films.
Teacher: Do you like reading?
Student: When I finish my homework, I always want to read. Without wasting a moment, I get my novel and I read. I never watch TV. So many programmes are so stupid. What a waste of time! My brother watches any programmes despite the fact that most are stupid.

Writing 1
What I like most is the security that a mobile gives you. It is the most useful thing in the world. My parents have just bought me the mobile that they had promised me. How lucky I am! You are never alone with a mobile and you can so easily call the police if you need to. Before going out, I always tell my parents that they can call me at any time. They are less worried. When I do my homework, with my new mobile I can surf the Internet in order to solve any doubts. In order to amuse myself, I send e-mails, I download video clips

and I play games. It does not make any noise and it has a five-megapixel camera that I can use at the scene of an accident or a crime.

We have the Internet at school. It is marvellous. It is an excellent way of communicating with friends and strangers all over the world. Besides that it allows me to use and practise foreign languages. Also, the Internet helps you to make new friends. I love music and I have an MP3 player that is really light, with a touch screen.

But I realise that there are disadvantages. Too many people spend too much time on their computers. They do less sport and after spending so much time at the screen they have eyesight problems. They are no longer interested in anything except their computers. They want to eat fast-food in front of their computers. They get lonely and sad and lose their friends. What a disaster! In order to help these people you have to limit access to the Internet. Mobiles are dangerous for your health, say the experts, because of radiation. Scientists are not sure. Be careful! Young people, without listening to the teacher, write texts during lessons. I have a girl friend who has been communicating with a stranger for a long time. What a bad idea! I need my mobile, I cannot live without it. Without it, life would be truly difficult but at the end of the month the bill is extremely expensive.

CHAPTER 4
Speaking 1

Student: Last year, I decided to go on holiday in June with my older brother. I wanted to visit my friends in Switzerland. They have been living there for two years. What a good idea! I think that Switzerland is the most beautiful country in the world because the mountains are superb.

Teacher: What was the weather like?

Student: It was nice weather and we went to the airport by taxi. We got on the plane and I found a seat. I put on my belt and the plane took off. I wasn't afraid.

Teacher: What did you do during the flight?

Student: Before catching the plane, I had bought a novel. I played cards and I read. We had lunch but the food was not good. It was chicken but I didn't like it. After eating, I felt ill. I arrived in Switzerland at six and my friends were waiting for me at the airport. They were very kind. We crossed the city of Geneva, we admired the lake and then reached the house. On arriving, we had a superb meal and we went to bed.

Teacher: Your impressions?

Student: The journey was very pleasant and my friends were very nice.

Teacher: And what will you do next year?

Student: My friends told me I must return to Switzerland to ski. I would like to ski because I love skiing so much and the snow is so good in Verbier. I would also like to go horse-riding because I have a horse here in England and I like horse-riding in spite of the weather. Last year, I went on rides in the mountains and I would like to do the same thing because I really liked it. There is a skating rink and a swimming pool in Verbier.

Writing 1

I am going to describe my stay in Blackpool to you. I have just spent two unforgettable weeks there. For me, Blackpool is the best city in England for holidays because there is always something to do. I was staying in a five-star hotel because my parents had won the lottery. It was superb because the swimming pool was always so empty! What luxury! They won a fortune so now we have bought a superb car and we stay at the best hotels. Fortunately my younger sister refused to come with us because she doesn't like Blackpool. She went to visit my grandmother.

In the mornings I walked on the beach. In the afternoons I played football in the park and in the evenings I went out with my parents. My parents told me to do a lot of exercise in order to keep fit. One day I decided to go to a theme park. On arriving, I saw the queues. It was terrible because the queues were so long. After waiting two hours, I was not happy. I was about to ask for my money back. I won't go to theme parks anymore.

In my opinion, the stay was excellent because we had a good time all the time and I was lucky enough to go out with a pretty girl/handsome boy. I often went out with her/him and we got on very well. It was fine weather every day. I would go back there without a doubt despite the long queues.

In summer, I will go to the USA and see my older brother. He has been living there for two years. I would like to see New York and he will come with me. I want to travel across the country to get to know it better. My brother will hire a car and off we go.

CHAPTER 5
Speaking 1

Teacher: What problems are there environmentally?

Student: We mistreat the Earth. What a disaster! Every year the situation gets worse. The people living in the developed countries use far too much energy. Each of us consumes the equivalent of 10 tonnes of coal a year. Man is an endangered species. We burn the forests which consume CO_2. In Brazil, they have burned thousands of square kilometres in a year. We pollute the air, we poison the rivers and the seas, we treat the planet like a dustbin, we modify plants and animals, we bury nuclear waste and we destroy our natural resources. The ozone layer is disappearing because of exhaust fumes. That causes the greenhouse effect and global warming. It is a vicious circle. We produce toxic gases which rise in the atmosphere. The heat of the Sun rises but is blocked by the gases. The Earth becomes hotter and hotter. The seas rise and lots of species are endangered. Our energy consumption is too high and the planet suffers.

Teacher: And what about flooding?

Student: The snow melts, the rivers overflow, the fields are flooded, the streets are under water. People are forced to leave their homes, the houses are ruined, the countryside is devastated and thousands are dead. Soon we will no longer have any fossil fuels.

Teacher: And the answer?

Student: The government closes its eyes to the problem. We have to change our habits, we have to have an action plan. We don't have much time left. We need to plant trees to replace the burnt forests. We must use public transport to reduce pollution. We should take showers, not baths, to safeguard the Earth's resources and to reduce water consumption. We must recycle everything. We must install solar panels and double glazing and insulate our homes. We should use bicycles to reduce CO_2 emissions and to reduce petrol consumption. The car represents liberty but also pollution. If we didn't use the car, we would use less petrol, and using the bus or the train we would pollute the air less, the air would be cleaner, we would take more exercise, we would feel better and we would be less stressed.

Writing 1

I do what I can in order to protect the environment. In spite of our efforts, our planet is on the brink of dying. What a disaster!

I cycle or I walk but I never go by car. I decided long ago to use public transport. I never throw litter. I even pick up litter in the park. I never waste energy. Before going out, I switch off lights and turn off taps. My parents have installed solar panels and double glazing and our house is so well insulated. After bathing or showering, I water the garden with the water I used.

When I speak to people, I encourage them to leave their cars at home. Cars represent liberty but also pollution. If we didn't use the car, we would use less petrol. We should use the bus and the train and we would pollute the atmosphere less, we would breathe clean air, we would take more exercise, we would be less stressed, and we would feel better.

In my house I tell everyone to recycle. I recycle cardboard, paper, bottles, plastic and packaging. I re-use plastic bags. We make compost with organic waste. I use rechargeable batteries to protect the environment. When I buy paper for example, I try to buy paper made from recycled materials. I give the clothes that I no longer wear to charity. Before buying something, I ask myself if I really need it.

I have written a letter to the Prime Minister. I told him we should reduce the amount of packaging per product, create more recycling centres, create cycle paths everywhere in our cities, plant trees in the streets and improve public transport. On top of that I told him to ban cars from town centres and ban free plastic bags. We should build fewer new roads and airports.

CHAPTER 6
Speaking 1

Teacher: What about your future plans?

Student: I have just done work experience and it has given me ideas for the future. I had to get up terribly early and I was working in an office. I had to photocopy, answer the phone, call customers and make the tea. At the end of this negative experience, I have decided that I never want to work in an office.

Teacher: Why?

Student: Because the work was boring. Several times I was on the point of leaving as the work was so boring. In spite of the fact that my colleagues were nice, I just wanted to go home. It wasn't the sort of work that I had been promised. The boss said I had to make the tea for the others. What a waste of time! It was an unforgettable experience. Fortunately, I have learned what I want to do and what I don't want to do.

Teacher: And that is?

Student: To start with, I am going to continue with my studies because I have seen that unqualified people have the worst jobs to do. Then I will go to university in order to get what I need to work in a profession. I have decided I don't want to work in the open air all the time and that I don't want to work in an office either. I am certain that I don't want to be a teacher. It is true that I dreamt of becoming a celebrity but I think that I want to become a journalist because the work is interesting, it is well paid and I would work in an office and outside.

Teacher: Are you going to get married?

Student: I will not get married before 30 and I will have three children. When I finish my studies, I hope to find a good partner. I will be happy because I will lead my life in the way that I have chosen. I will live in a luxurious house and will continue to work whilst my partner stays at home.

Teacher: Marriage is important?

Student: Marriage helps us to have a harmonious relationship. It is something that unites the couple. I am going to get married because it is important for children to have stability.

Writing 1

I am fed up with my school. They are not giving me the quality of education that had been promised to me.

I have been a student here for four years and I find the school day very stressful and I am on the point of getting ill from it. I am just a name on a list. The school rules are unreasonable, it is forbidden to wear make-up or jewellery, give opinions, smoke, eat or drink in class etc. When I get up, I have to put on an ugly, frightful uniform. Although it is good for discipline, it is ugly and not very elegant. Everybody looks the same. It is the worst school in the area.

The atmosphere in my school is terrible. There is violence and graffiti. Extra-curricular activities do not exist. Some students make too much noise and I cannot hear the teacher. The football pitches are too small and there isn't enough equipment. What a disaster!

I don't get on well with my teachers because they are not interested in me. They explain nothing, they don't listen to us and don't understand us. They give us too much homework. I have a language teacher who has no authority and who cannot prepare good lessons. I understand nothing in those lessons.

Despite the fact that I haven't the time to do everything asked of me, my parents put me under too much pressure without realising. I work all the time and don't have time for leisure. I must get good marks all the time. I fail everything, I don't make progress and my results are disastrous. I have decided to do A-levels but unfortunately to do them I need good marks. I would like to go to another school and I have just asked my parents if it is possible.

Listening transcripts

CHAPTER 1

Speaking 1 (track 2)

Listening 1 (track 3)

(a) Una botella de vino tinto, por favor.

(b) Un café con leche, por favor.

(c) Para mí, pescado.

(d) Quiero una cerveza.

Listening 2 (track 4)

Camerero: ¿Una mesa para dos personas? Hay una mesa aquí en el rincón, lejos de la ventana abierta. Les voy a traer el menú del día. Primero déme el paraguas. Tenemos una tortilla muy buena pero no tenemos mariscos. Sólo tenemos tortilla de jamón.

Cliente: Voy a pedir una tortilla pero de primero quiero una ensalada. Y de postre no quiero nada. Y de beber quiero vino tinto.

Listening 3 (track 5)

Cliente 1: Buenos días. Déme mariscos, por favor. Y una cerveza.

Cliente 2: Hola. Quiero patatas fritas, por favor. Y un vaso de leche.

Cliente 3: Buenos días. Quiero pescado. Y un zumo de naranja.

Cliente 4: Quiero un bocadillo de queso y un vaso de vino.

Cliente 5: Déme un helado. Y un café solo.

Listening 4 (track 6)

Tu problema no tiene nada que ver con lo que has comido. No tiene nada que ver con el sol y la playa tampoco. ¡El problema es que te acuestas muy tarde todas las noches! ¡Y bebes demasiado!

Listening 5 (track 7)

Isabel: Oye, Antonio, ¿quieres un cigarrillo?

Antonio: No, gracias – no fumo.

Isabel: ¿Por qué no?

Antonio: La ropa de la gente que fuma huele mal y además a mi novia no le gusta. Dice que es una cosa poco saludable.

Isabel: Pues yo empecé a fumar a la edad de quince años.

Antonio: ¿Por qué empezaste?

Isabel: Pues, salía entonces con un grupo de jóvenes que fumaban. Yo hacía como ellos. Ahora fumo más de veinte cigarrillos al día. Para mí es un placer y no quiero parar.

Antonio: ¿Qué dicen tus padres?

Isabel: Como los dos fuman también no dicen nada. Me dejan fumar pero no en casa. Si quiero fumar tengo que salir fuera.

Antonio: Pero cuesta mucho dinero, ¿no?

Isabel: Sí, pero como trabajo en casa de una señora limpiando la casa tengo bastante dinero.

Antonio: Y ¿bebes alcohol?

Isabel: Nunca en mi vida.

Listening 6 (track 8)

Section 1:

El dependiente: ¿Qué desea?

El hombre: Un kilo de manzanas y medio kilo de uvas.

El dependiente: ¿Y para usted?

La mujer: Cien gramos de jamón y una botella de leche.

Section 2:

El dependiente: ¿En qué puedo servirle?

El hombre: Quiero una barra de pan y una bolsa de caramelos.

El dependiente: ¿En qué puedo servirle?

La mujer: Déme unas flores y una caja de cereales.

CHAPTER 2

Speaking 1 (track 9)

Listening 1 (track 10)

(a) ¿Mi familia? Pues, soy hijo único pero tenemos dos gatos.

(b) No vivo con mis padres. Vivo con mi hermano mayor y mis hermanitas.

(c) Mis padres han muerto. Vivo con mi abuela.

(d) ¿Detalles de mi familia? Pues, vivo con mis padres y mis dos hermanas.

(e) Yo vivo con mi hermano y tenemos dos perros.

(f) Me gustaría tener un hermano pero tengo solamente una hermana.

Listening 2 (track 11)

– Hola. Me llamo Juan. Odio todas mis asignaturas menos el arte. Me encanta el fútbol pero no me gusta el tenis. Normalmente voy al instituto en bicicleta. No me gusta ir andando.

– Buenos días. Me llamo Elena. Me gustan casi todas mis asignaturas pero no me gusta la historia. Mi favorita es el inglés. También me encantan todos los deportes menos el tenis. Me gusta especialmente el baloncesto. Por la mañana mi padre me lleva al instituto en coche porque el autobus es caro.

– Hola. Me llamo Sofía. Nací en Francia así que me gusta mucho el francés pero mi asignatura predilecta es el alemán. Mi hermano me da clases de natación porque él es profesional pero yo prefiero el ciclismo. Es peligroso ir al instituto en bicicleta así que tomo el autobús.

– Buenas tardes. Me llamo Enrique. Quiero ser químico así que paso mucho tiempo haciendo química. Las otras asignaturas – el inglés, etcétera – me aburren. Me encanta el hockey. No me gusta el fútbol. No hay autobuses así que voy al instituto andando.

Listening 3 (track 12)

No tenemos tiempo para poner tus cosas en tu dormitorio. Vamos a comer en seguida. Después vamos a ver tu dormitorio. No te preocupes. Está muy lejos de los ruidos de la calle. No hay mucho espacio en tu dormitorio porque la cama es grande pero puedes poner tus cosas en el armario. Si quieres comer aún tenemos un poco de bacalao. Y después vamos a salir a una discoteca con otro amigo inglés. Y al volver estará mi hermano y puedo presentaros.

CHAPTER 3

Speaking 1 (track 13)

Speaking 2 (track 14)

Listening 1 (track 15)

– Oye, Alfonso, ¿quieres salir esta tarde?

– Lo siento pero no puedo...es decir que ya he quedado con mi novia: vamos ahora a patinar. Luego vamos a comer en un restaurante. Después vamos al cine y por último vamos a una discoteca. Lo siento, pero no tengo tiempo.

– Hola, Jaime, ¿quieres salir esta tarde?

– Lo siento, no puedo. Tengo exámenes dentro de dos meses y tengo que estudiar. Si no apruebo no puedo ir a la universidad. Voy a estudiar durante todo el día todos los días. Lo siento, pero no puedo salir.

–¿Qué tal, Ana? ¿quieres salir esta tarde?

– Lo siento, pero no tengo tiempo. Esta mañana voy a misa. Luego voy a ayudar al sacerdote a limpiar la iglesia. Después tengo que visitar a los enfermos en el hospital y más tarde tengo que escribir a los periódicos quejándome de la pobreza que existe en algunos barrios de esta ciudad. No, no puedo salir.

Listening 2 (track 16)

Pablo habla de su día

Voy a pasar el día con una amiga muy especial. Se llama Conchita y nos conocemos desde hace mucho tiempo: íbamos a la escuela juntos. Como mi madre tiene que dar clase sería mejor no almorzar en casa y conozco un sitio que ofrece los platos que a Conchita le gustan. Luego como ponen una película de miedo en el centro de la ciudad iremos a verla. Y más tarde como a Conchita le gusta bailar iremos a 'La Mariposa' hasta las diez de la noche.

Listening 3 (track 17)

Carla: Oye, Fernando, vamos a ver una película. Yo quiero ver una película de miedo. Son mis favoritas.

Fernando: Las películas de miedo no me gustan. No quiero ver esa película.

Carla: Entonces, ¿qué quieres ver?

Fernando: Yo prefiero una película del oeste. Son mis favoritas.

Carla: Una película del oeste...me da igual, pero ¿no sería mejor ver una película de amor? Me gustan bastante.

Fernando: Si vas a una película de amor, vas sola. Ni hablar. Pero si quieres me gustaría mucho ver una película de aventuras.

Carla: Bueno. Una película de aventuras...si quieres ...supongo que sí.

Listening 4 (track 18)

En Lima hay mucho interés por todo tipo de deporte pero sin duda el más popular es el patinaje sobre hielo. Es un deporte nuevo pero entre los jóvenes es más popular que el fútbol. En algunas zonas se puede jugar al golf: todos los clubs aquí están dirigidos por profesionales. En el centro de la ciudad se encuentra la Piscina Nacional y es famosa porque el equipo olímpico del Perú se entrenó allí. El equipo de baloncesto del Perú también es muy famoso porque hace dos semanas ganó una medalla de oro en un campeonato en Nueva York.

Listening 5 (track 19)

Estás escuchando un servicio automático para los clientes del cine Astoria. Hoy y mañana solamente ponemos una película histórica llamada *Corazón de acero*. Es una película americana con subtítulos. Pasado mañana durante siete días ponemos una película de terror llamada *Los muertos*. Trata de unos fantasmas en una casa antigua en Inglaterra. Finalmente, a partir del 23 y hasta final de mes, ponemos *No me toques*, una comedia que ganó un premio en Italia. Hay tres sesiones para cada una de las tres películas, a las dos, a las siete y a las doce.

Listening 6 (track 20)

Sótano: Joyería, Fotografía, Equipaje

Primera planta: Deportes, Relojería, Ropa de caballeros

Segunda planta: Música, Ropa de señoras, Electrodomésticos

Tercera planta: Comida, Fruta, Legumbres

Listening 7 (track 21)

Puesto 1: Habas, zanahorias, cebollas, patatas...y ¡qué precios! Nosotros tenemos los precios más bajos de este mercado.

Puesto 2: Muñecas, coches eléctricos, juegos, trenes, juguetes...ofrecemos productos de la mejor calidad.

Puesto 3: Mesas, sillas, sillones, armarios, camas...y el transporte a tu casa es gratis.

CHAPTER 4

Speaking 1 (track 22)
Speaking 2 (track 23)
Speaking 3 (track 24)
Listening 1 (track 25)

– Buenos días, señora.

– ¿En qué puedo servirle?

– Pues, he perdido mi mochila.

– ¿Me puede usted describir la mochila?

– Sí, es azul y bastante grande.

– ¿Qué contiene?

– Dinero, las llaves del coche y mi pasaporte.

– ¿Dónde la perdió?

– Creo que fue en el mercado.

– ¿Cuándo la perdió?

– Ayer.

Listening 2 (track 26)

(a) Quiero escribir a mi amiga Isabel pero no encuentro un sello. ¿Dónde están los sellos?

(b) Voy a comprar un regalo para Isabel. Voy a comprarle un libro.

(c) Esta tarde voy a salir a hacer deporte. Mi deporte favorito es la natación.

(d) No sé dónde está mi dinero. ¡Ay sí! Lo he dejado en mi dormitorio.

(e) Cuando salga con Isabel vamos a visitar el puente romano.

(f) Compraré el regalo en el Corte Inglés. La librería está en la segunda planta.

(g) Voy a ir al centro en autobús. El autobús sale a las diez y media.

(h) Isabel me dice que se va de vacaciones a Turquía en avión.

(i) Isabel me dice que va a pasar todo el día en la playa.

(j) Isabel me dice que va a volver el cuatro de agosto.

Listening 3 (track 27)

Señoras, señores, estamos llegando a Barcelona y estaremos en el hotel en media hora. En unos momentos pasaremos cerca de la catedral – podrán verla a la izquierda – pero no tenemos tiempo para visitarla ahora. Esta tarde la cena en el hotel será de nueve a diez y media. Voy a poner un vídeo mostrando los sitios de interés en Barcelona. Mañana por la mañana volveremos allí a verla con más tranquilidad. Y mañana por la tarde tienen tiempo libre para conocer la ciudad e ir de compras. Pasado mañana nos marcharemos a Zaragoza y pasaremos tres días allí. Bueno señoras y señores, espero que el hotel les guste y si tienen algún problema marquen el número tres para poder hablar conmigo.

CHAPTER 5

Speaking 1 (track 28)
Listening 1 (track 29)

Valencia está en la costa mediterránea y es importante porque tiene un puerto. Muchísimos barcos usan el puerto todos los días. A muchos ingleses les gusta vivir en Valencia por su clima. Casi nunca nieva en invierno. Hay fiestas magníficas en febrero y muchos turistas visitan Valencia en ese mes.

Listening 2 (track 30)

Buenas tardes, éste es el pronóstico del tiempo para hoy lunes, mañana martes y pasado mañana miércoles. Hoy lunes habrá un viento glacial con chubascos fuertes. Mañana martes habrá un cambio porque las nubes van a desaparecer y se prevé tiempo soleado y estable todo el día. El miércoles se prevé otro cambio porque los vientos y el frío van a volver, ocasionando lluvias intensas en todas partes.

CHAPTER 6

Speaking 1 (track 31)
Listening 1 (track 32)

– Me llamo Pedro. Estoy harto de mi instituto. Muchas veces le digo a mi madre que estoy enfermo para poder quedarme en casa. Y a veces con ciertos profesores no voy a las clases: me quedo en el café. La única cosa que me gusta es...bueno...las vacaciones.

– Me llamo Pilar. Me aburro en el instituto aunque voy todos los días. Me fastidia lo que tenemos que hacer. Sólo hay una asignatura que me guste: la clase de geografía. Es que el profesor es tan guapo.

– Me llamo Enrique. Me encanta ir al instituto. Aprendo muchísimo y me gustan todas mis asignaturas menos una: geografía. No me entiendo bien con el profesor. Lo curioso es que un día quiero ser profesor de geografía.

Listening 2 (track 33)

José: A mí no me gustan los idiomas. Prefiero las ciencias, sobre todo la biología. Me interesa la biología porque el profesor es muy joven e interesante. Un día quiero ser médico y me gustaría trabajar en el extranjero. En mi tiempo libre me gusta patinar. Hay una pista de patinaje cerca de mi casa.

Lolita: No me gusta la historia en absoluto. ¿Sabes por qué? Los libros que usamos están muy pasados de moda. Mi asignatura favorita es el francés. Voy a Francia todos los años de vacaciones. Un día quiero ser profesora de francés. Mi hobby favorito es la lectura. A veces leo tres o cuatro novelas a la semana.

Listening 3 (track 34)

¿Desempleado? ¿Por qué no trabajas para La Compañía Rovi? Buscamos representantes que puedan trabajar en Oriente Medio. No pagarás impuestos y el alojamiento será gratis. Llámanos.

Index